THE WELCOMING PARISH

Donal Harrington

The Welcoming Parish

the columba press

First published in 2005 by
the columba press
55A Spruce Avenue, Stillorgan Industrial Park,
Blackrock, Co Dublin

Cover by Bill Bolger
Origination by The Columba Press
Printed in Ireland by ColourBooks Ltd, Dublin

ISBN 1 85607 482 X

Table of Contents

Introduction

In one way or another, welcome is key to all that is positive and creative in the life of the parish. It is fundamental to how people are thinking and feeling today. The sentiment formulated in one parish captures it: 'God's heart is a welcoming heart, reaching out in Jesus to embrace all; our parish dream is that all would feel welcomed and called to welcome.'

It may be that welcome is the primary form of what John Paul II calls the 'new evangelisation'. 'Evangelisation' is literally about communicating the good news of the gospel. But the word itself can be off-putting. People appreciate that it is a subtle thing. They sense that it is more about welcome and belonging than anything else. Welcome creates the experience of faith community from which all else follows.

The twenty-four chapters that follow explore different aspects of the welcoming parish. The early chapters reflect on what parish is all about and on the spirit that inspires it. These are followed by a number of chapters on ministry and leadership in the parish. Finally there are ten chapters on specific areas in which parishes practise the ministry of welcome.

Throughout the chapters there is a back-and-forth between theory and practice. On the one hand, the best practice in today's parish brings forth the best of theology. On the other, good theology is the foundation and inspiration for good practice. Much of my focus is on how we think about the themes and issues in parish life today.

By way of thanks, I limit myself to one name, that of the late Father Paddy Wallace, to whom I dedicate this book. Parish renewal in Ireland owes him so much for his originating vision. It was a blessing to have worked with him.

CHAPTER 1

Why Parish?

Everybody knows what a parish is. Whether everybody knows what it is meant to be is another matter. Everybody would know a parish if you pointed it out to them, but do we know what a parish is in its essential purpose?

Tied up with this is the fact that 'parish' means different things to different people. Sometimes in a group, I begin discussion with a brainstorm of the associations the word 'parish' has for people. Here is a sample of what comes up:

Territory	*People*
Priests	*Frustration*
Community	*Money*
Hard seats	*Identity*
Stations	*Holy water*
Football team	*Heritage*
Confirmation	*Jealousy*
Belonging	*Worship*
Politics	*Family*
Christmas crib	*Personalities*
Insular	*Mass cards*
Funerals	*Schools*

The list reflects people's memories, a mix of nostalgia and pride, warmth and disillusion. The list also reflects something of people's vision and hopes. In this, it offers a glimpse into the essential purpose of the parish.

Over the next few chapters we will be reflecting on that purpose – on the aim and mission of the parish. Back in 1963, Pope Paul VI had this to say: 'I believe that this old and respected structure of the parish has an indispensable mission of great contemporary importance.' It is a great expression of hope in a new and bright future. These chapters seek to unfold something of that hope.

The territorial parish
However, not all would agree with what he says. Some would hold that parish is more a thing of the past than a thing of the future. They would say that tomorrow's church will take different forms and that parish belongs to a form of church that is becoming obsolete.

There may be different reasons for people holding this view, but a prominent one would be related to the words 'territory' and 'boundaries' in the brainstorm above. Here 'parish' is an organisational word. It refers to an administrative unit, like a branch office of a multinational. (Interestingly, in that comparison, it's what goes on at the centre that matters; branch offices can be closed down!)

We all see how this form of parish is breaking down today, especially in urban areas. People do not identify with their local church in the way that they used to. People 'shop around' and the place where they worship may not be the place where they live. Increasingly we have 'non-resident parishioners'.

Indeed, where people worship may not be linked to parish at all. It may be more about a group of people, from all kinds of different places, whose 'common denominator' is not where they live, but some shared interest or experience. Tomorrow's church, it is argued, will be characterised by people belonging to small groups with a vibrant shared sense of discipleship.

Some advocate that we should move our resources into what is known as 'sector ministry'. Sector ministry is ministry where people are. For years we have had chaplains (more recently, pastoral teams) in hospitals and schools and prisons. Now we are seeing this kind of practice extend to such places ('sectors') as shopping centres, industry and business.

It is worth mentioning here also the phenomenon of what

might be called non-geographical parishes. In our now multi-cultural society there is a growing ministry specifically for ethnic groups that is not tied to a parish territory. Similarly, in the Dublin diocese, there is the Parish of the Travelling People which is diocese-wide and transcends geographical boundaries.

In ways such as these, the grip of the territorial parish is loosening. Faith community and geographical community do not necessarily coincide. Alongside this is another trend: that as more dioceses go down the road of strategic planning, pastoral strategies will be multi-pronged. There will be strategies that do not have the traditional parish as their focal point. There will be a communications focus; there will be an education focus; there will be a social justice focus; there will be a youth focus; and so on. And there will be a parish focus.

In this future, parish will be one focus among many. It will continue to be a focus. But it will not be the only focus of pastoral strategy in a diocese. And yet, I would suggest, it will be the core focus. Even as neighbouring parishes work more and more together as pastoral units, the individual parishes within that larger unit will endure. Let me explain why.

The faith community
Pope John Paul II once said that the parish is 'not principally a structure, a territory, or a building, but rather the family of God, a fellowship afire with a unifying spirit, a familial and welcoming home'. In the light of the above trends, this stands as a challenging perspective.

It means that the parish is to be seen as *people*. Of course it is other things as well. It is an administrative unit. It is a provider of services. It is, normally, a geographical area. But this is all the background. In our understanding of parish, the foreground is occupied by people. I recall speaking with a Chinese priest who was saying that, with the widely scattered Christian communities in his country, the parish has no buildings – just people.

As an image for this point, think of watching a dance. We can be captivated by dance – the charm of the movement, the elegance, the rhythm, the vitality, the gracefulness. But if we could see through all that – perhaps with an X-ray camera –we would see, beneath the skin of the dancer, the bones and sinews, skeleton and muscles. It is the fine-tuning of all this structure that makes the dance possible, but the structure itself is invisible.

The quotation above is an invitation to think of parish as the dance – and to think of the structures as in the background. The structures and buildings, the organisation and administration aspects, are not primary. They are at the service of people. They are there to enable the dance. But how many, who look at parish and church, see the dance? How many see only a structure?

Some people today suggest that we adapt our language accordingly. Perhaps 'parish' has too many institutional connotations. Perhaps a term like 'faith community' would convey more of what we want the word 'parish' to say today. Such an alternative would better capture the spirit of the thing. As well, it would allow us think in terms of a number of faith communities within a pastoral area, without being bound by territorial considerations.

Church

A reflection on the word 'church' fits in well here. 'Church' has even stronger connotations than parish of the structural and institutional. Yet, when it was first used by the earliest Christians, it had no such connotation at all. It meant something like 'the gathering'. 'Church' – *ekklesia* – meant the followers of Jesus, gathered in a particular place, to break bread together in memory of him.

This may sound simple but it is hugely significant. The basic response to revelation, to what God has done in Christ, is 'church'. What do you think is the basic response to God's revelation? You might say; to accept it with joy. Or to be converted and repent. What is missing in such responses is that they are 'I' not 'We'. The basic response to the Christ event is to *gather*. To gather is to remember; to remember is to break bread together; and out of that we can give ourselves to 'earthing' the gospel in the way we live and the place where we live.

This is the heart of what parish is about. Not a branch office, but the mystery of 'church' actually happening or being realised in this particular place and time. 'Parish' is what 'church' is – a faith community, people of faith who gather together – the basic response to God's communication in Christ. This links in with the reality of parishes which have more than one church. Those parishes might better be described as pastoral units comprising a number of distinct Eucharistic communities or gatherings.

Community

In this, the parish stands also as a counter-statement to a trend in contemporary spirituality. People's deep 'spirituality' expresses itself in very varied ways today – many of them a real challenge for the church to learn from. But one of the negative aspects is a privatising tendency, a tendency to see spirituality as a private affair between 'me and God', with no reference to or need for community. Perhaps this reflects a more widespread tendency to 'privatise' that characterises capitalist culture.

The parish is a statement that Christian spirituality is not a private affair. It is a statement that the basic response to Christ is not to repent or pray, but to gather. The basic response is to be together. Christ is the morning light shining in our world. When we experience ourselves as 'enlightened', we also become aware of the others who are sharing the same experience. We do not turn inwards, but we gather. That is where Christ is found.

In this, the parish is responding to the deep human need for community. For all our prizing of freedom and autonomy, we know that human becoming is not possible outside of community. Aristotle offered the comparison of the pieces on a chess board. Each has a meaning, a context. But apart from the chess board and the other pieces, any piece is lost. All too many people are like that, engaged in a very lonely spiritual struggle.

Thrown together

It is, of course, true that the experience of Christian community may be had apart from the parish. This leads us to appreciate a further aspect of what is at the heart of the parish.

Someone once remarked that, in a world that seems to be growing more divided, the parish is 'one of the few open communities in which rich and poor, educated and uneducated, upwardly mobile and sheer down-and-out can meet and call each other brother and sister.' The remark is somewhat idealistic and is contradicted by the divisions that can exist in parishes. And yet it contains a truth.

The truth is this: because the parish is a geographical unit, it has a 'thrown together' quality. Just as you do not choose your family, so you do not choose your fellow parishioners. They are all shapes and sizes, diverse not uniform. And in a sense that is the glory of the parish. It makes very real the words of Paul to the Galatians: 'There is no longer Jew or Greek, there is no longer slave or free, there is no longer male or female; for all of you are one in Christ Jesus' (Galatians 3:28).

This would be lost if Christians gathered only on the basis of shared interests or experiences or age-group – if, in other words, Christian communities were communities of the like-minded. There is something in the thrown-together nature of the parish that testifies to our radical equality and to the breadth of what is embraced and encompassed in the Body of Christ.

Assurance of care
One further aspect of what is at the heart of the parish. While the territorial parish goes back to the early centuries of Christianity, its final developments came with the Council of Trent and the Counter-Reformation. There, the whole of the church was organised systematically into territorial units, each under the care of a pastor.

This, as I understand it, was not out of any obsession with organisation. It was a reaction to a situation where clergy were often absent from their place of appointment. It was an effort to ensure that every Christian would be able to say, 'this is where I belong'. From now on, each Christian would be able to point to somebody who was responsible for him or her, a representative of the church whose responsibility it was to be available and at their service.

In this sense, the very existence and structure of the parish is an assurance of care for each individual Christian. Whether you or I actually worship in our local church does not take away from this fact. In the structure of the parish, the church as a whole has committed itself to care for me. The parish as such is a statement to me, 'we care that you exist.'

CHAPTER 2

The Last Supper

Each of the gospels of Matthew, Mark and Luke, in their record of Jesus' last night, recount the event of the breaking of bread. The gospel of John, the last to be written, does not. Instead it tells us about Jesus washing the feet of Peter and the others – an event to which the other three evangelists do not refer. And yet, even though there are two stories, there is a single meaning.

One connecting link is that both actions are accompanied by a command. After washing the disciples' feet, Jesus says to them, 'If I your Lord and Teacher have washed your feet, you also ought to wash one another's feet.' And after sharing the bread and the cup, he says to them, 'Do this in remembrance of me.'

The commanding links the two actions together as two sides of a coin. In fact, as we shall see, they are even more intimately linked than that. Together, the two actions eloquently express what is the heart of the parish, the two essential dimensions of what it is and what it desires to be – a family of people who break bread together and who wash each other's feet. As they do, they remember Jesus and keep his memory alive. As they do, Jesus lives and acts in their midst.

In order to appreciate Jesus' own meaning, we might recall the context. This was somebody who was about to die. This was his last occasion together with his friends. When we ourselves recall friends who have died, we know that dying words and gestures have a special import, whose significance continues to increase as they are remembered afterwards. The significance multiplies when those words and gestures have been deliberately chosen.

This was the case with Jesus. On his last night, he deliberately chose these two actions to gather together or 're-member' his whole life. They were to be the recapitulation or culminating expression of what he believed and of who he was. It was as if everything he was and everything he stood for was concentrated into these two symbolic actions.

But why these two? Why wash somebody's feet? Why share bread and say, 'this is my body'? Where did he get the ideas? I would like to speculate on where the ideas came from and thereby fill out something of their meaning.

Giving and Receiving Ministry

To understand the foot washing, I would like to go back to the very beginning. Jesus' public ministry, as we call it, was immediately preceded by his time in the desert. This time was pivotal. It was a time of resisting allurements and setting his sights, a time of fundamental choices and life-decisions. It was a time of huge struggle and turmoil. Mark's account concludes by saying that angels came and 'ministered to him' (Mark 1:13).

That is extraordinary when we think of it. The first thing, before Jesus ever 'ministered', was this – his being ministered to. We are used to thinking of Jesus giving ministry. We are not used to thinking of him as receiving ministry or needing to be ministered to.

Later on in the gospels there is another instance. Jesus is in Bethany with his friends Martha, Lazarus and Mary. At the meal, Mary took some very expensive perfume and anointed Jesus' feet and wiped them with her hair. The house, we are told, was filled with the fragrance of the perfume (John 12:1-8).

There are variations of the incident in the other gospels. In Luke's gospel Jesus is eating in a Pharisee's house and it is a sinner woman who enters. She starts to bathe his feet with her tears and to dry them with her hair. Then she continues kissing his feet and anointing them with ointment (Luke 7:36-38; see also Matthew 26:6-13 and Mark 14:3-9).

The sensuousness of the moment is forcefully conveyed. Just

imagine that it is yourself instead of Jesus, your feet in place of his! But again, it is Jesus being ministered to. Somebody notices him, appreciates him, takes care of him.

Is it too much to suggest that all this forms part of the background to the last supper? Jesus prepared carefully and thoughtfully for that occasion. He reflected and decided what he would do. And the idea for what he would do – to wash the feet of his friends – did not come out of the air, but from the experience he had had himself.

Such a scenario echoes with our own experience. Some of our best insights into the meaning of ministry – of love and care and service – have come to us, not from what we have done, but from the ministry we have received. Likewise with Jesus. In this action he wanted to say that life is essentially about the giving and receiving of ministry. So much so that he tells Peter, 'Unless I wash you, you have no share with me.' And his inspiration came, at least in part, from what he had received himself.

Table Fellowship

It is worth noting that the incidents recounted above took place in people's houses, at table, in the context of a meal. A very significant part of Jesus' own ministry was at table, such that his 'table fellowship' is one of the practices most revealing of who he was and what he was passionate about.

He was not exclusive about his table companions. He is frequently in the company of Pharisees. But mostly he is seen associating with what the gospels refer to as 'tax-collectors and sinners'. These were people with messed-up lives, whose sense of alienation had been multiplied by their being judged and ostracised. It is like when others do not believe in you and you internalise that and the circle is complete. Their hearts were sunk, their lives were in a cul-de-sac, they no longer saw their own beauty.

What Jesus did was simple and profound. He shared table with them. From our own experiences of meals, we know that to share table is not functional but symbolic. Getting fed is not breaking bread. To share table is to share lives. It is welcome and solidarity. It is full of belief and hope.

That was the experience of these people. The smile returned to their faces as they rediscovered their humanity. One such person was the sinner woman mentioned above. As she bathes and kisses Jesus' feet, it is the love in her heart that is pouring forth – love that was locked in and which was released through Jesus' sharing of table with her. That is what Jesus means when he says, 'her sins, which were many, have been forgiven; hence she has shown such great love' (Luke 7:47).

What Jesus did is complemented by what he said and visualised. He imagined the kingdom of God to be like a banquet where everybody is included (Luke 14). In sharing table, Jesus is enacting what he imagines. In his table ministry, 'kingdom' is happening.

Last Supper

We come back, then, to the last supper. Why do we call it the 'last' supper? Presumably because it was Jesus' final supper before his death. But it was also 'last' in the sense of being the last in a long line of such meals. It was not an isolated, once-off event. It was quite typical; it was what he had been doing again and again over the previous years.

But at this, his last supper, because he knew it was his last supper, he wanted to gather together and focus all that had gone before. When he took bread and said, 'this is my body, for you', he was crystallising what he had been doing all the time, and so often at table – giving ministry, giving hope, giving life.

If we now recall the other action, the foot washing, we can legitimately ask; are there two actions or one? For both are symbols or 'sacraments' of service. Both are statements that life is essentially the giving and receiving of ministry. Both are saying that God's own self is completely invested in this vision.

Parish

Parish is about the intimate connection between these two actions.

It is about the faithful following of these two commands. To wash one another's feet in the giving and receiving of ministry, and to break bread together at the table of the Lord – these are the two cornerstones of Christian community. In our daily lives we minister to one another. In our Eucharist we experience the ultimate act of ministry – God's ministering to us, which is the secret meaning of all our ministering to one another.

An acquaintance of mine recounts an experience that brings this meaning to life. This is the story as she tells it herself:

My husband John was distressed when he phoned me. His twin sister Mary had arrived in Dublin and her drinking binge was now into its third day. Mary's drinking problem of fifteen years had taken its toll on her family, especially her husband and three children. They were finding it hard to cope and were relieved to see Mary go to Ireland to give them a chance to recover from the stresses and strains of living with an alcoholic.

'What will I do with her?' John asked me, his voice full of emotion reflecting his frustration, sadness and despair. 'Bring her here,' I said, 'We'll take it one hour at a time.'

Mary was a sorry sight when she arrived at our house. This elegant beauty that had once turned many a man's head now looked so frail and helpless. All I saw was a weak and tired little girl clutching a Duty Free bag that contained her 'soothers'.

Our silent embrace spoke volumes. This was no time for words. Mary didn't need a lecture; she needed water and a comfortable bed. While she slept we cleared our house of drink for fear she might be tempted. But we needn't have bothered. She had had her fill of drink – three days was enough!

The following day was relatively quiet with the family taking it in turns to keep vigil. Our five year old was happy to do more than his fair share of shifts … and I can still see the touching sight of the two of them on the sofa together watching 'Home Alone'.

From a safe distance, concerned family members phoned to enquire 'Is everything alright?' That was as close as they could bear to come. By Saturday Mary was on the mend. Despite reassurances from us that she was 'very welcome' and 'no trouble at all', we could sense her embarrassment and humiliation.

By Sunday Mary was well enough to come to Mass with us. We knew the Gospel Choir at the 12.30 would really lift her spirits and they didn't disappoint. The music and singing on that sunny Sunday morning was just what the doctor ordered as we sat together as a united family.

Fr Tom read the gospel and, incredible as it may seem, it was the story of 'The Rich Man and Lazarus'. About a wealthy man who dressed in expensive clothes and lived in great luxury and a poor man named Lazarus, who was covered in sores and lay at the rich man's gate. But the rich man was oblivious to the plight of poor Lazarus and did nothing to relieve his suffering.

I glanced over at Mary and I could see that she was crying. I'm sure she realised, as we did, that she was a modern day Lazarus but, in this case, she hadn't been ignored or forgotten.

After Mass a large crowd of parishioners gathered outside the church for a chat. Fr Tom came up to us and said, 'You know, I was just wondering where John got the beautiful redhead?' With a warm handshake Mary was now 'a welcome stranger to our community'.

That evening we received word that an elderly neighbour had died. The following morning Mary and I went to the shop to buy bread, ham and eggs to make sandwiches. While we buttered the bread we talked about Mary's drinking problem and her pain. We didn't fix anything, but it helped to talk without judgement! I know Mary felt good making those sandwiches and sharing them with our neighbours in need.

A single mystery

A woman experiences having her feet washed. In church, she comes face to face with the mystery of ministry, as Jesus says, 'my body, my life, for you', as the priest breaks the bread at the table. Later she is washing a neighbour's feet. Breaking of bread and washing of feet; everything that a parish is and is meant to be. Jesus ministering to us, and we ministering to one another; all making up a single mystery.

A few years ago in the parish of Greystones, they built a family centre right next to the church. Before he died, the parish priest Paddy Wallace had a painting commissioned for the connecting corridor between the two. The painting had two panels, one of the last supper (nearer the church), the other with the washing of Peter's feet (nearer the centre). Linking the two was a ladder, harking back to Jacob's ladder and rising up to the light of God.

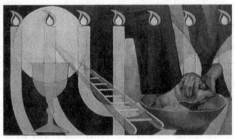

He composed a prayer in which he linked the painting with the parish's vision statement:

As Jacob saw constant movement up and down the ladder
linking the light of heaven with the affairs of the earth,
so we will be led towards God's light in our own lives
when we try to live out our vision statement
of caring for one another in the way Jesus taught us –
celebrating Eucharist together and washing each other's feet.

The parish church and the family centre. Celebrating the Eucharist and ministering to one another. Twin aspects of a single mystery of connecting with the light of God in our lives – the mystery of what parish is.

CHAPTER 3

A Ministering Community

Ask yourself the question, what is a parish for? What is the aim of the parish? The question is as simple to ask as it is challenging to answer. It is as important as it is overlooked. And yet, what we prioritise and attend to in our parishes is a consequence of how we understand the aim of our parish. In addressing the question, I will be building on the reflections of the previous chapter.

A Meditation
I want to begin with a mental exercise that takes up from the theme in the last chapter of giving and receiving ministry. Relax yourself and think of a time when you yourself were ministered to – when you received ministry from another. It might be something that has been very significant for you or it might be something quite ordinary. It might have happened recently or it might be from long ago.

Whichever it is, choose a memory and begin to replay the tape. What were the circumstances in which you found yourself? Who was it that ministered to you? What was their ministry? – perhaps something they did, or something they said. As you re-live the occasion, reflect on what this ministry meant to you and what it did for you.

When a group of people engages in this meditation, there is a great richness in what comes up. For instance, somebody re-counts an experience from thirty or forty years ago that continues to mean much to them. Somebody else describes how hard it was for them to allow themselves to be ministered to. Even the most ordinary of moments, like somebody giving way to you in traffic this morning, assume a special quality.

You could go on to a second mental exercise that reverses the situation – where you recall and reflect on an occasion when you yourself ministered to another. You could compare the two experiences, of giving and receiving ministry. We say that it is better to give than to receive, but that does not mean that it is easier to give than to receive. Peter's reaction at the Last Supper tells us as much. Yet, if you do not allow yourself to be ministered to, neither do you allow the other to minister.

The aim of the parish

This is one way of talking about the aim of the parish. The exercise captures something of the heart of what a parish is all about, namely, the giving and receiving of ministry. 'Ministry' is a word we rarely use in this way. Usually it suggests something churchy, or else something quite different, such as government ministries. But the exercise makes 'ministry' into something that we can all identify with and recognise in our own lives.

Ministry is going on everywhere – in every home, in every relationship – wherever there is an encounter between the need of one person and the giftedness of another. Most ministry is unnamed, inconspicuous, untrumpeted. It would not even think of itself as 'ministry'. And yet, wherever and whenever it happens, people are obeying Jesus' command, 'you also ought to wash one another's feet'. Whenever it happens, there is the event of 'grace'.

As a parish this is what we are and what we are meant to be – a ministering community. Our daily giving and receiving of ministry is our realisation, or 'earthing', of what the gospel is all about. And when, in obedience to Jesus' other command, we gather for the Eucharist, we are placing all our ministering in the context of the ultimate act of ministry, which is God's ministering to all humanity in the death and resurrection of Jesus.

A sea change

This is what parish was always meant to be. From the beginning, faith-community has meant ministering community. About twenty years after the resurrection Paul was writing to the church in Corinth in just these terms. The different way in which each of us is 'gift' is a unique manifestation of the Spirit. In this Spirit we are one body – so much so, that if one suffers, all feel the pain; if one rejoices, all share the joy.

John Paul II speaks in the same vein of 'solidarity'. Solidarity is about the duty of all towards all. In solidarity we are each committed 'to the good of all and of each individual because we are all really responsible for all'. Ministering to one another in the Spirit of Jesus both witnesses to and deepens our solidarity as the Body of Christ.

At the same time, to speak of ministry in this way reflects a profound transformation – a sea change – in how we understand and speak of ministry. The change has come about over the last forty years or so, since around the time of the Vatican Council.

Around the time of the Council, 'ministry' meant 'priest'. Ministry was something that priests did – and it was something that priests did *for* people. Ministry was a one-way relationship, where priests ministered and people received ministry. This focusing of the idea of ministry on the activity of the priest is not original. What is original is the thinking of Paul just quoted. But the narrowing of focus began within a century and prevailed for most of the history of the church until now.

For the past forty years the focus has been broadening. The first folk groups were around the late 1960s. Since the same time we have had qualified lay religious educators. Our first ministers of the Eucharist were commissioned in the late 1970s. Then there are ministers of the word, baptism teams and bereavement groups, prayer guides and caring ministries, and so on. All the time there has been emerging a richer and richer variety of 'ministers' – and thereby of ministry – in the Christian community.

The thrust of all this flowering reaches further. The thrust has been towards a sense of the ministry of all, not just of some. It is inspired by a sense that baptism, not holy orders, is the primary sacrament of ministry, the original 'ordination'. We are all called to ministry, to ownership, to share responsibility – because we are all really responsible for all.

We could say that there are three moments in the sea change. First there is our inherited sense that ministry is about ordination. Then there is the emerging sense that ministry is also about the different ministries exercised by lay people in the faith community. Thirdly there is the sense that ministry is about all being engaged as a ministering community.

We speak today about 'collaborative ministry'. But soon we will be speaking of it no longer. When we are aware of ourselves as a ministering community there will be no need for the word 'collaborative'. We will know that it is already contained in the word 'ministry'.

The provided-for church
At least that is the theory. It is a new way of seeing ministry, and indeed it is quite extraordinary the number of people who have entered into the new way of seeing in such a short period as forty years. But it still has to filter through much further. Most of our church still has not made the shift.

One reason is that we have had a 'provided for' mentality, where ministry is something that is provided for us by priests. This is not surprising when we consider the sheer number of priests – not to mentions religious sisters and brothers – we have had to minister to us. One friend recounts how, in his leaving certificate class around 1950, over half the boys went on to the seminary! That is the way it was; we were 'spoilt', so to speak. No wonder we would think of ourselves as 'provided for'.

The danger here is that, when lay ministries appear, the 'provided-for' mentality does not change. The lay ministers are a kind of extension of the priest – the providing-for goes on. And when the number of priests falls, and parishes are reduced in personnel, people ask, 'who will provide for us now?' This seems to be the pattern worldwide. If a pastoral council or a lay leader is proposed in response, people feel sorry for themselves for a while, but then they get used to this new way of being provided for.

Another aspect of this is that the lay ministers themselves

sometimes see themselves as an extension of the priest. They see themselves as there to help him do his job. Compare the situation where you call a plumber to the house. You stand nearby as he works away under the sink. Then he asks you to pass him the wrench. Does that make you a plumber? No; you are just helping him to do his job.

In ministry it is the other way around! We are not there to help the priest do his job. He is there to help us. The whole role of the priest, as understood in today's church, is about activating the ministry and priesthood of all the baptised. He is the enabler, the midwife, the moderator, the orchestrator of a ministering community. As Cardinal Mahony of Los Angeles put it, the members of the Body of Christ *should recognise themselves* in the ministry of the ordained.

Private religion
Another reason why the 'ministering community' mindset has not filtered through has to do with a weakened sense of solidarity in the faith community. We can now see that much Christian piety in the past was quite privatised. While the priest 'said' Mass, people said their own prayers and rosaries. Each was engaged in their own private devotion. People resented the sign of peace as an encroachment on this. Even still, some older people resent music after communion as an intrusion into their private prayer. More generally, religion has been something we keep to ourselves.

This is disappearing, but something equivalent has emerged instead. Today people sometimes say that what they like about Mass is that it is their 'quiet time' during the week, when they can stand back, reflect on things, experience some peace. There is something lovely about that, but note the language – it is *my* quiet time. An acquaintance in the Church of Ireland remarked to me recently that all their Sunday gatherings are diminishing – except in the cathedrals. Cathedrals are in the centre of towns and cities; you can go there and have your own 'quiet time', anonymous and undisturbed.

You might call it spirituality without community. I have already commented on a tendency to the private in contemporary spirituality, but this is a novel angle, to think that people within the churches can be content with spirituality without community. If this is accurate, then our gathering may be no more than our being alone together! We may have to acknowledge that oftentimes it may not be a community that is 'celebrating the Eucharist', so much as a collection of individuals, engaged in private acts of public worship.

Baptism and the Body

The preceding reflections lead me to the topic of baptism. The more I reflect on the renewal of the parish, the more I find myself thinking that baptism is the key. There is no difference, I would suggest, between the renewal of the parish and the appropriation or re-appropriation of our baptism.

The key question is: what does it mean to be a layperson? What does it mean to be baptised? What does it mean to be a disciple? This is where the so-called 'vocations crisis' is located. The deep crisis is not when there is a shortage of priests, but when large numbers of baptised people have little sense of what it means to be a follower of Christ. The significance of this phenomenon has led John Paul II to speak of the 'new evangelisation', which we shall discuss in the next chapter.

Here I wish to highlight one central aspect of what it means to be baptised. The following is an excerpt from a sermon of Saint Augustine. As the bishop, he was speaking after Easter to the newly baptised. The final step in their Christian initiation was initiation into the meaning and mystery of the Eucharist. He begins his sermon with the question, how can the bread on the table be the body of Christ and the chalice his blood. He continues:

'If you wish to understand the body of Christ, listen to what the apostle says to the believers, "You are the body of Christ and his members." If, therefore, you are the body of Christ and his members, it is your own mystery that has been placed on the table of the Lord. It is your own mystery that you receive. To this which you are you respond "Amen" and, in responding, you accept it. What you hear is "the Body of Christ" and to this you respond "Amen." So, be a member of Christ's body, that your Amen may be true ... Be what you see and accept what you are.'

This sermon, when I first came across it more than two decades ago, was a revelation. Before then, if I had heard the term 'body of Christ', I might have thought of the physical body of Jesus on the cross. I might have thought of the host on the altar. But here was a third meaning. *We* are the body of Christ. The body of Christ is on the altar; the body of Christ is in the pews.

Baptism means: this is the mystery of who I am. I am a member of the body of Christ. I am a manifestation of the Spirit, gifted for the enrichment of all. I am part of a unity where all are really responsible for all. I am a valuable member of a ministering community.

As a child I learned to kneel down and close my eyes after receiving Holy Communion and to join my hands and pray. More recently I have learned to spend some moments at this time sitting up and looking around, as people go to and come from Communion. During those moments I think, 'This is the body of Christ.' And I say, 'Amen.'

CHAPTER 4

Welcome

It has become very clear to many that the theme of welcome goes to the heart of what the parish is and what the parish aspires to be. The theme of welcome is replete with inspiring and challenging perspectives for the parish's self-understanding today. The theme connects us in a very deep way with what the gospel is all about.

'Gospel' is an old English form of 'good news'. The writers of the New Testament gospels are called 'evangelists', meaning people who proclaim good news. Two thousand years on, the faith community is the primary place where the good news of the gospel is proclaimed and experienced and celebrated. And we are learning to appreciate that welcome is at the core of these processes.

An intuition
It is instructive to attend to the language which people in parishes use when they try to articulate their aim as a parish (what we call mission or vision statements). The language that predominates is about people feeling that they belong; about a sense of inclusion that can accommodate each and that embraces all; about people being accepted where they are at, irrespective of their views, no matter who they are; about people feeling at home; about people feeling valued and wanted and cared for; about welcome and hospitality and outreach; about people feeling equal and important.

The recurrence of this language in parish after parish represents a very strong intuition about what a parish is. It is saying that the parish belongs to all; so therefore, all should feel that they belong to it. It is mine; it is ours; it is us. In part, the intuition is formed by a familiarity with people who do not feel this welcome – people who feel excluded; people who have been hurt; people who feel unworthy; people who cannot connect. These people are not faceless. They are our family, our friends. It is this that imbues our intuition with such passion.

The most life-giving initiatives in parish life today are about welcome. Some parishes have invested seriously in preparation programmes for communion and confirmation and for baptism. Many of the people encountered on these occasions are not Mass-goers, but the programmes are linking with them at very special moments in the lives of their families. The whole thrust of the effort is that the link would be an experience of joy and welcome and affirmation.

The same is true of many other initiatives. The work of bereavement teams and funeral teams; the creativity and imagination of family-friendly Masses; ministers bringing communion to the housebound and the availability of parish Mass on radio; the communal form of the Sacrament of Reconciliation; a team of parishioners visiting the homes; and so on. All this focus means that people are having an experience of church that is not an experience of 'being told' or of 'being bored', but an experience of welcome and warmth.

God's heart
It is remarkable how loudly this resonates with the gospels. When we open the pages of the gospels with welcome in mind, we find that the theme is there waiting for us, page after page.

Welcome is at the beginning of the gospels. Mary says, 'let it be' and welcomes Jesus into her body and into her life. The shepherds welcome, the Magi welcome; they are all delighted to hear good news. But there is also a darker side. Herod says to the wise men, 'When you have found him, bring me word, so that I may also go and give him homage.'

The pattern continues through the life of Jesus. On one hand, he is welcomed – 'a woman named Martha welcomed him into

her home'; Zacchaeus 'hurried down and was happy to welcome him'. On the other hand, in contrast, John the evangelist
says, 'He came to what was his own and his own people did not
accept him.' Jesus himself says, 'I have come in my Father's
name and you do not accept me.' He tells the story of the tenants
who plan to kill the heir and gain his inheritance.

But the hub of the gospels is about Jesus welcoming us.
'Come to me,' he says, 'all you who are weary and are carrying
heavy burdens and I will give you rest.' The Pharisees and
scribes grumble that he repeatedly 'welcomes sinners and eats
with them'. 'Let the little children come to me,' he responds in-
dignantly to his disciples, 'do not stop them.' 'And he took them
up in his arms, laid his hands on them, and blessed them.'

The heart of Jesus is full of welcome and his welcome is
boundary-breaking. It reaches out beyond 'his own'; it is inclusive, all embracing. He heals the Roman centurion's son. He responds to the persuasion of the Canaanite mother. He engages
deeply with the Samaritan woman.

In all of this, Jesus is representing and embodying God's welcoming heart. In the story of the great banquet to which all are
invited (eventually!) and in the story of the prodigal son, he
imaginatively symbolises the way in which welcome is the heart
of God. He proclaims that the good news is that God's heart is a
welcoming heart, reaching out to embrace all.

Our heart

Finally, the good news calls us to participate in Jesus' ministry.
Just as Elizabeth welcomed Mary, so we are called. According to
Paul, we are 'to welcome one another just as Christ has welcomed you'. We are told more than once by the New Testament
writers to 'extend hospitality to strangers'. When we welcome
others, we are also welcoming Jesus. 'I was a stranger and you
welcomed me ... just as you did it to the least of these, you did it
to me.'

Likewise Jesus tells his disciples, 'whoever welcomes you
welcomes me and whoever welcomes me welcomes the one

who sent me.' We are always to have a welcome in our heart for good news and for its bearer. Perhaps, though, the bearer is not always somebody we would have expected.

This leads in to the story of Dives and Lazarus, where Jesus gives us a chilling sense of how we can fail to welcome. 'There was a rich man who was dressed in purple and fine linen and who feasted sumptuously every day. And at his gate lay a poor man named Lazarus, covered with sores, who longed to satisfy his hunger with what fell from the rich man's table.'

The moral is clear. What is at the heart of God is what must be at the heart of the church. Welcome is to be the very heartbeat of the faith community. Then we will be an effective sign of God in the world, making the good news known.

Catching up on God

It is vital to remember that welcome originates in God's heart. It is firstly what God is doing in the world. The 'good news' is God's 'evangelising' the world. God is testifying in Jesus as to the welcome for humanity that fills God's heart.

In the power of the Spirit, this good news has now gone out to the whole world. When we remember that welcome is originally what God is doing, we acknowledge that God has gone on ahead of it. We, the faith community, do not bring God's welcome to people. We follow after it. Sometimes we trail far behind it and we try to catch up and to appreciate that God's welcoming heart is bigger than our imagination.

God is already so much there in people's lives! People often say that they are not 'religious'. They may not even use the word 'God'. They may just speak about their children, their plans, their garden. At the same time their talk is full of faith and hope, thanks and prayer. There is such commitment to what they believe in. There is such passion about values like love and integrity. There is such a basic trust in life and its mystery and its meaning, often in the face of cruel adversity.

As a faith community, our 'take' on this is that grace is already there. We are called to proclaim the good news, but that does not make us sole distributors of God's grace, as has been conceived. Proclaiming good news is mainly about recognising God's grace and welcoming it with joy where we see it already ahead of us. Might that be part of the meaning in Jesus' parables of the treasure in the field and the pearl of great price?

The church first learned this very early on, in struggling to appreciate that the good news was for the Gentiles as well as the Jews. The Acts of the Apostles (chapter ten) tells the story of Peter coming to realise that God's Spirit was working in the Gentile Cornelius. Peter did not convert Cornelius. It was Peter who was converted, as is indicated by his own conclusion, 'who was I to withstand God?'

Good news is a two-way process

The implications for parish, and its understanding of welcome and outreach, are immense. When we talk today about 'mission' and 'evangelisation', it is almost ingrained in us to talk as if it were a one-way process. We might not put it so crudely, but we often think in terms of 'we have what they need'. This is the legacy in us of the paternalism and condescension which have coloured the history of how our church has understood mission and grace.

In our time, John Paul II has stressed what he calls the 'new evangelisation'. Traditionally, he says, mission meant bringing the gospel to parts of the world where it had never been proclaimed. Now a further meaning has emerged. In lands long Catholic there are increasing numbers of people who have been baptised but who have little or no familiarity with following Christ. This turns things right around. Hitherto mission was about the unbaptised; now it is also mission to the baptised!

The challenge of what is said above is to see this as a two-way process. The best of contemporary thinking about mission sees it as dialogue. Nobody has a monopoly on God. As somebody put it, we need a mission-centred church, not a church-centred mission. If we are centred on God's own mission, God's evangelising the world with the good news of God's own welcoming heart, then we enter into dialogue with the other. The other is 'holy ground'. In reaching out we enrich and are enriched in turn – because it is God who is acting, not us.

Making connections

There is a very strong sense today of the need to make connections between Christian faith and people's lives. There is a gap, a distancing. The language and thought-forms and rituals are often failing to connect.

But again, it is a mutual process. It is not as if, on one side there is 'faith' and on the other there is 'life'. People's lives are already full of faith – and hope and love. It is more about making connections between this 'faith' and what we used to call 'The Faith', between the gospel story of God and the story of God that is each human life. (A small boy is said to have remarked, 'People are the words with which God tells his story.')

It is as if the world is the forum of God's welcoming, saving, affirming, redeeming activity – and the church is the place where that activity is given a name, is revealed for what it ultimately is. As a faith community, we do not so much bring something to the world as offer to the world the name for what it is already graced with. And that is the connection.

But the key step is welcome and friendship. It is the fundamental and irreducible way of proclaiming good news – the good news that is already in the world. As John says, 'He was in the world, yet the world did not know him.' Words will come later. Eucharist will come later. Welcome and acceptance come first.

There could be a temptation here to think of welcome as a means to an end – as if we present a smiling image of the church in order to draw people in; as if we welcome in order to then evangelise. That is an untruth. Welcome is not a means towards evangelising. Welcome *is* the evangelising. It *is* the good news of God's all-inclusive embrace.

The hidden energy

Pope Paul VI once asked, with a note of perplexity, 'In our day, what has happened to that hidden energy of the good news, which is able to have a powerful effect on the person's conscience? To what extent and in what way is that evangelical force capable of really transforming the people of this century?'

In our parish faith communities today we are searching for this energy. We have been blessed with an intuition that, in putting welcome first and reaching out in welcome, we will be put in touch with that energy. In reaching out we will find that we ourselves are being evangelised.

CHAPTER 5

A Feeling of Home

The word 'church' has a bad feel for many people. It is about a personal experience of hurt or condemnation. It is about fear and guilt. It is about authoritarian teaching that seems to have little conception of what it is to be an autonomous adult human being. It is about obscure argumentation whose connection to the real world is hard to grasp. It is about teachings that lack credibility because they fail to square with experience. It is about the scandal of those occupying the 'high moral ground' not being all that they seemed.

That this is not the whole picture hardly needs to be stated. It does not include all that is positive and prophetic in the Christian vision. Nevertheless, what we are describing is a significant strand and it deserves to be acknowledged as a cause of both pain and alienation. Part of the mission of the parish today is to be a place where this pain is addressed and this alienation healed.

Clubs and Rules

There is, of course, the view that the problem does not lie with the church at all, but with individual people. One way in which this view is expressed is in the image of the 'á la carte Catholic'. This image is meant to describe people who see their own conscience as the arbiter of right and wrong and who believe and do as they themselves please. They pick and choose from amongst the teachings of the church according to personal preference.

This is quite a powerful image but one which, on reflection, is quite objectionable in what it implies both about individual disciples and about the church itself. It implies, first of all, that anybody who diverges from what the church teaches is a casual Christian whose moral behaviour is a matter of following whims and who regards the teaching of the church as being about as weighty as today's newspaper editorial.

This is a considerable injustice to the very many who find themselves at variance and who are far from casual in their discipleship. Their lives are characterised by a deep relationship with Christ and a strong attachment to the Christian community. Their being out of step with the church on a particular moral issue is a source of great concern and agony, so much so that many would sooner cease the practice of their religion than feel themselves hypocrites by going to church while still out of step. Indeed, their discipleship may often be a far more inspiring witness than that of many who have no particular issue with church teaching at all.

Secondly, the image of the 'á la carte' Catholic implies an image of the church which is woefully inadequate and which, because it remains implicit, is allowed to fester. It suggests that the church is like a club or an organisation where, on joining, people are presented with the rules and told that if they do not like any of them they are free to go elsewhere instead. It is 'the whole package or nothing'.

This is what the image implies and some would say that it captures something that is actually true of the church. The image suggests a group that tends more to exclude than to include, a group more interested that people conform than that they belong. If it is true at all, what perhaps is most sad about it is that the image is so impersonal. It suggests no bond at all of intimacy between the person and the church, no prior family affinity, but instead a cold, clinical transaction.

The church itself might want to acknowledge that it has been guilty of this way of being. But what is deeply wrong with the image of the 'á la carte' Catholic is that it implies that this is what the church should be like all the time. It says that the church should be hard and strict about rules and regulations, that it should treat people according to the law, and that it should keep its membership pure. The question then is: is this what the church is meant to be and if not, what it is meant to be like?

The church as home

An alternative image is to see the church as 'home'. In exploring
this image I am thinking of the parish as the place where people
can have this alternative experience of church.

The image is already there in the passage quoted earlier
where John Paul II spoke of the parish as 'the family of God, a
familial and welcoming home'. I realise that, because of their
own personal experience, not all will warm to the image of
home. So I pursue the image without trying to idealise 'home',
in acknowledgment of that reality.

The spirit in which the image of home is intended is captured
well by Robert Frost in his poem, 'The Death of the Hired Man'.
There it says:

'Home is the place where, when you have to go there,
They have to take you in.'

'I should have called it
Something you somehow haven't to deserve.'

Home is where a person always belongs, where there is always a
place at the table, where belonging does not have to be earned.
This is true even for the black sheep of the family, though there
may be a process of time involved. Gradually, eventually, while
things may never be what they used to be, people will come to
break bread together again.

It is unnatural, though understandable, if this does not come
about. Imagine a man whose marriage has been a disaster. After
the parting of ways he comes to love another. They decide that
they will live their lives together. Imagine that this man's mother
cannot accept what he has decided. She is so unable to accept it
that she may not have anything to do with him again, even to
the extent of eliminating his name from her conversations. It is
almost as if he had ceased to exist. Imagine her going to her
grave like this.

We can appreciate the deep pain here. At the same time we
can recognise that it would be so unnatural, so much the opposite of what home means. A feeling of home is a feeling of something that is so basic that it is able to negotiate its way through

almost anything. It may take time, but the truth of 'home' is that it can rise above and assert its supremacy.

The village fountain

To speak of the church as home is to see the church as always open to be big enough for those who belong to the family. It is to see the faith community as what John Paul II described as 'a house of welcome for all and a place of service to all'. In the same passage he went on to quote Pope John XXIII's image of the parish as 'the village fountain' to which all might have recourse in their thirst.

This way of thinking may make for a messy rather than a tidy place. It will not be conducive to a membership consisting only of the pure and worthy. There will be a varied membership, including the wounded and the damaged, the imperfect and the inadequate, the sinner and the failure, as well as people with differing perspectives. It will be open to all who in their thirst are drawn to the village fountain.

Such a home would be a place of hospitality. The emphasis would be on inclusiveness rather than exclusion, on ensuring that all would feel welcome, no matter what their situation, and that all would sense that they belong. An attitude of exclusion would want to check the credentials of all before they enter, to see where they have been. Hospitality would sit everybody down. Turning up at the door would of itself signal the disposition that gains entry. Hospitality would look to the future rather than the past.

Gospel echoes

If we refer this line of thought back to the gospels, the story of the prodigal son comes to mind. Usually it is understood as a story of God's mercy, a mercy which precedes and embraces our repentance. Perhaps, in the context of the present discussion, it may also be taken as an image for church and parish. Hospitality, arms open in anticipation because, quite simply, this is one of our own coming home.

We might develop this imagery further by suggesting that the elder son in the story represents another image of church, one that is closer to that implied in the idea of the 'á la carte' Catholic. Here hospitality, as well as the sense of family, fade into the background as he objects: 'But when this son of yours came back, who has devoured your property with prostitutes ...' Everything is defined by the past and a price will be exacted before there is any entry.

The story presents a choice. Which church do I want? Which church do I believe in? It is not a choice between integrity and bending over backwards to accommodate anybody and everybody. It is a choice between what is and what is not gospel. The mindset of the welcoming parish allies itself firmly with the father in the story.

This may seem to imply that anything goes. What of those whose lives are a positive contradiction to the Christian vision? What of those who come casually, uncommitted, yet expecting the same access as anybody else, to the sacraments for instance? Obviously such cases demand a thought-out response. The point, though, has to do with the fundamental attitude which the image of home conveys, that of thinking in terms of inclusiveness and belonging, thinking in terms of 'this is family'.

It should also be noted, however, that the supposedly cynical disposition of the so-called 'á la carte Catholic' does not at all represent the disposition of most of those we are talking about. Generally, those who are anywhere near the door and desirous of belonging are far from cynical or hypocritical. They are at least as single-minded in their commitment as others who sit comfortably inside by the fire.

Listening

Home is a place where parents are attentive to all that is going on in the lives of their children. Ideally there is time spent individually with each child, whereby each has a sense that his or her story is both known and cherished. There are places – like the kitchen table – where difficulties are worked through and

where, when something has been messed up, the sense of threat
is eased by the assurance of care.

If the church is home for all its disciples, it likewise attends to
what is going on in their lives. As with the kitchen table in the
household, there is a sense of wanting to discuss things that happen to people. People have a sense that their experience counts
and has authority. Complementing this and because of this, they
have a deep respect for the collective wisdom of the faith community.

An image that it may be helpful here is that of the potter and
the clay, an image with which the Bible expresses something of
our relationship with God. 'Just like the clay in the potter's
hand, so are you in my hand, O house of Israel' (Jeremiah 18:6).
There is something about this image that we resist. It makes it
appear as if we are totally dependent, completely pliable, without self-determination. It contradicts our sense of ourselves as
mature, responsible Christians.

It is good, then, to listen to what a potter would say about the
imagery. If you and I were potters, we would know as potters to
respect the clay in our hands. We would not just do as we wanted
with the clay. But we would hold the clay in our hands and
allow it to speak to us. We would listen to the clay and allow the
form to emerge, to speak itself to us. While always able to mould
and remould the clay, we would always respect the material
that is under our hands.

If this is an image for God and ourselves it means that God
listens to us intently and respectfully. In the silence of God we
are given space to speak and what we say matters to God. But if
this is an image for God and ourselves, then it also has something to say about the parish and ourselves. It says that attentive
listening to the life experience of God's people is at the heart of
what goes on in the parish. When we feel listened to we feel dignified. When we feel our experience is noticed we feel important.
When we feel accepted where we are at, we start to feel at home.

CHAPTER 6

Deciding Together

A welcoming parish is characterised by a strong sense of owner-ship. Feeling that we belong is also a feeling that this is our parish. But if it is our parish, that also has implications. It means that we are responsible for ourselves It means that we decide for ourselves what to make of ourselves. It means that we decide to-gether.

The issue here is not so much about what decisions are made in the parish as about how decisions are made. How decisions are made is a reflection of how the parish is as a faith community. Decision making is different in a parish that understands itself as a ministering community than it was in the 'provided-for' parish of the past.

A new culture

Traditionally decision making has been a priestly affair. More accurately it has been the preserve of parish priests; even curates may not have got a look-in! That was simply part of the under-standing of ministry as something that priests do for people.

Recent decades have seen the introduction of parish pastoral councils and with them has come a modified understanding of decision making. The actual phrase used in canon law says that the pastoral council has a consultative voice only *(consilium pas-torale voto gaudet tantum consultivo)*. It is not a legislative or deci-sion making body. Its conclusions have the status of counsels or suggestions to the parish priest.

This may seem clear, but its meaning needs to be teased out. Some have interpreted it as meaning that the council is 'merely advisory'. One parish priest set up a council with precisely this motivation – 'I don't have to listen to them'! What should be clear, however, is that decision making in today's church is meant to be different than it used to be. In proposing pastoral councils and such like, the Vatican Council was proposing a new, more participatory form of church.

But it is not about replacing one form of 'ministering-to' with another. In the past the priest did all the deciding. To replace that with a pastoral council doing all the deciding changes very little. It still remains a faith community where everything is decided 'for' them. Decision making in today's parish is meant to be something we all do together, as part of expressing the truth that we are all really responsible for all.

A pastoral perspective
The place to begin is with theology, not with law – with pastoral rather than legal perspectives. This is suggested by the word 'consultation' itself. The fact is that, with Vatican II, the thrust in the church has been in the direction of a more and more consultative ethos – parish pastoral councils, diocesan pastoral councils, diocesan priests councils, synod of bishops, and so on. Consultation is not about a minimalist form of collaboration. It is about what Pope Paul VI called a 'new habit of mind', a mindset of participation and partnership.

What we are talking about is not so much a legal point as a spirituality. We are growing as church in a spirituality of partnership. This spirituality is rooted in Jesus' words to the disciples at the last supper; 'I do not call you servants any longer, because the servant does not know what the master is doing; but I have called you friends, because I have made known to you everything that I have heard from my Father' (John 15:15).

In this perspective we are all 'insiders', partners with one another, partners with God. The Holy Spirit speaks through each one of us, not just through the clergy and hierarchy. The basic relationship in the church is not between clergy and laity, but between friends. We are engaged together as friends in seeking out the will of God. That is what 'consultation' means.

Cardinal Newman remarked that, when he 'consulted' the barometer, he was not looking for an opinion but rather the truth about the weather. Consultation is a search for the truth, a search for what God's Spirit is saying. If the Spirit speaks through each of us, then consultation can only happen when there is an intent listening to what each one is saying. Without that listening the Spirit may not be heard.

An ethos

This implies that decision making in the parish is grounded in a whole ethos of mutual interaction. Concretely this means that the parish will only get its decision making right when it gets the right interactive ethos.

Pope John Paul speaks of that ethos as 'the ability to see what is positive in others, to welcome and prize it as a gift from God'. In such an atmosphere people are listening to one another, hearing what each other says, building on each other's contributions. Differences are taken seriously, as an invitation into a richer perception of the truth. Members of the faith community are learning to trust one another and are growing in a shared vision.

We know the enemies of such an ethos. The dominant group or dominant character who prevents others from participating. The kind of 'listening' that is so preoccupied with getting in its own point that it cannot hear what is being said by others, let alone build on it. Personal agendas and hidden agendas that will not entertain a larger vision or a collective wisdom. The complacency that is not open to change.

The ethos I am describing is one where seeking the collective wisdom and hearing what the Holy Spirit is saying converge. The more the thrust is towards finding the collective wisdom, the more the Spirit is speaking. The stronger the enemies of collective wisdom, the more the Spirit is muted and chained.

In the beginning

It should be becoming clear that decision making is not the preserve of the priest. It is not even something that the priest does with the pastoral council. It is something that the parish does for itself.

The parish is a ministering community, where all are really responsible for all. This has to be reflected in how decisions are made. One former Irish President was said to have 'looked into his heart' to discern what the people of Ireland needed. That is not the model we are talking about, where the priest or the pastoral council would look into their heart, as it were, to see what the parish needs. There has to be a real sense that the parish is making decisions for itself.

There is something of this spirit reflected in two major decisions of the church in its earliest days. In Acts 6 there is a decision to give the Hellenist Christians their own leaders. In Acts 15 there is a decision to accept the Gentiles without imposing on them the law of Moses. Both are part of the gradual and painful opening up of Christianity beyond Judaism.

In both cases the twelve apostles preside over the decision. But in both cases the process is one where the whole community of Christians is called together. The problem is discussed, a solution is proposed and the multitude join with the twelve in giving their approval.

Here is a model, right from the origins of Christian community. No doubt it is easier to imagine it happening in a community of one hundred people than in one of three thousand. But the heart of the model is a sense of ownership on the part of the faith community, an ownership that is reflected in a participative style of decision making.

In practical terms, this is not to propose that every parish decision has to be referred to the whole parish. But it does imply that decisions have to be made *with reference to* the whole parish. A group such as a pastoral council is not making decisions *about* the parish; it is making decisions *on behalf of* the parish. It is the parish that is 'in charge' of itself. And it is in the parish as a whole that the truth is to be found, for the parish as a whole is where the Holy Spirit acts.

Parish assembly

A simple way to engage the faith community in taking this kind of responsibility for itself is to set up some form of parish assembly. I say 'some form' because it can take different shapes.

It could be an annual parish assembly. This assembly would be facilitated by the pastoral council. It might begin with a review of the year gone by – not just what the council has been doing, but how the faith community has been during that time. This might lead into some discernment as to what should be the priority areas to attend to in the coming year. This in turn might be expressed in an inspiring theme for the year.

It is important that such an assembly is not called an 'AGM' – an annual general meeting for most people is something you avoid! Some prefer not to have it at exact annual intervals for this reason. The assembly is not about motions and elections. It is a forum that seeks to deepen our sense of our shared care and responsibility for our faith community.

That sense will not emerge overnight. A parish assembly may well attract quite a disappointing number of people. Lots of those who are very involved in the parish might not turn up. It is because we are not used to this way of doing things. It will take years to build up an assembly to the stage where it really reflects a sense in the faith community that we are really responsible for our own parish and our own future.

Some parishes and dioceses prefer a more frequent form of assembly – if not involving the whole parish, at least a sizeable representation of it. Where this is do-able it obviously makes for a greater participation of a larger group of people in the ongoing decision making processes in the parish.

Even still, it is rarely possible to have everybody involved all the time. That makes ongoing communication vital. Newsletters, notices, websites, contact with parish groups are all aspects of building up effective lines of communication between parish leadership and the community at large. People will grow in a sense of ownership if there is ongoing information about what is happening, together with opportunities to respond.

All the time, meanwhile, there is fading away into the background the sense that parish is a place where things are decided and done 'for me'. It may be worth adding that a parish where there is a pastoral council, but little in the way of communication channels with the faith community as a whole, is going to struggle to achieve a wide sense of ownership of decisions that are made.

The way of consensus
It may be appropriate to say something about the mechanics of making decisions, whether at a parish assembly or a pastoral council. The above perspectives point to 'consensus' rather than voting as the way of decision making in the parish.

To explain what consensus means, picture a gathering discussing the best time of year for holding a parish open day. Some strong voices are advocating the autumn; one or two quieter types timidly suggest early summer; others again have not spoken. The facilitator asks for a comment, one by one, from everybody, to get a sense of the meeting. It turns out that there are more who favour the early summer date. It also emerges that some people feel the time is not yet ripe for an open day.

Consensus is first of all about listening to everybody, which will often demand 'hearing people into speech'. It is about the equality of submerged voices and dominant voices. The first step in consensus is knowing that everybody has been heard. Now the Spirit has been released. It is clear from the example how this might never happen and how the views of a few could be mistaken for the collective wisdom of all.

The next step is taking each other seriously. There will be majority voices and minority voices. If I am in a minority and the majority take me seriously, I am inclined to take the majority seriously in turn. But taking each other seriously may mean retracing ground, going back over why some people see things differently. In sharp contrast, there's a story about a parish meeting where a vote was taken and one person jumped up shouting 'we won'!

The next step again is not unanimity, but consensus. One or two of us may end up saying, 'I don't agree with the majority view, but I'm happy that I have been listened to and heard, and I'm happy to go along with the prevailing view.' Note the language – not 'I'll reluctantly and resentfully give way' but 'I'm happy'. Consensus is not about some people feeling they have compromised their position. It is about a sense of 'win-win', not 'win-lose'. That can only happen within a spirituality of partnership.

The priest

Even though decision making is participatory, it is not accurate to speak of the priest as just another person in the process. He is appointed by the bishop to the care of this faith community and he is the one who is answerable to the bishop for the affairs of the parish. Being a priest does not mean that he comes with extra graces of wisdom, but it does mean a role and a place that requires specific acknowledgment.

The priest also has a crucial enabling role as the leader of the community. The contemporary theology of priesthood highlights the particular calling of the priest to call forth and activate the ministry or priesthood of all the baptised. As leader he initiates and encourages the journey towards a collective wisdom. He more than anybody must believe in the convergence of the Spirit's speaking and the group's articulating its collective wisdom.

In this context some have spoken of the priest as 'confirming' or 'ratifying' or 'sanctioning' the consensus in the gathering. This is intended, not in the sense of permission-giving, but of recognising the working of God's Spirit in the working of the gathering and thereby of reassuring the gathering in its ownership.

If it happens that the priest's is a minority view on a particular issue, then consensus is lacking in a special way. In such a context two things are required. On the one hand, the priest should be very slow to act against a consensus on the part of the rest of those assembled. On the other hand, those assembled should be very slow to want to act despite the views of the priest.

Rarely, if ever, will the prospect of the priest's veto power become an issue when the spirituality of partnership is truly at work. This again reiterates the key point regarding decision making. The key is the spirit in which decisions are negotiated, the 'how'. An ethos that welcomes all God's people to exercise their shared responsibility is the foundation for getting the decisions right.

To conclude, decision making in the parish is evolving through three stages. A first stage is where it was the preserve of the clergy. In a second stage decision making is shared within the context of the parish leadership group. But the third stage is what we are aiming for where the faith community experiences itself as a ministering community that is deciding for itself what to make of itself.

CHAPTER 7

Planning for the Future

Today, the main kind of deciding together that the faith community needs to engage in is about planning. It is critically important to its survival and flourishing that the parish learns to plan for its own future. In this regard, it is very significant how John Paul II highlights planning in a recent document:

'We must set about drawing up an effective pastoral plan. It is in the local churches that the specific features of a detailed pastoral plan can be identified – goals and methods, formation and enrichment of the people involved, the search for the necessary resources – which will enable the proclamation of Christ to reach people, mould communities, and have a deep and incisive influence in bringing gospel values to bear in society and culture.'

It should be stressed that planning is an activity of the whole faith community. It may be guided by the pastoral council or some other group, but it needs to engage with the parish as a whole. It is common wisdom that the successful plan is the one built out of people's own dreams and perceptions, where there is a lot of 'buy-in', a lot of ownership. Otherwise, people can legitimately say: *whose* plan? *whose* vision? *whose* priorities? Without ownership it remains a 'provided-for' parish.

Some are suspicious of planning language, feeling that spirituality and strategy do not sit well together. But in fact they are in harmony. As we shall see, God's reaching out to us in Jesus is very much about God 'planning'. To integrate 'strategic planning' into our spirituality brings this to the fore. It represents a convergence of the 'professional' and the 'professing'. Planning adds a professional dimension to a professing community.

Managing change

The language of planning today has a specific meaning. It is more than the ordinary planning we do, as when we plan our holidays, or when a teacher plans a class, or when a parish plans a special ceremony. Planning in the more specific sense is recent, because it is about managing change, and managing change is a relatively new challenge. When times change, something new is needed beyond what is already there.

A typical reaction to change is to go on as before. A small business says, 'This is the way we have always done it.' A parish priest says, 'I wasn't trained for this.' People and organisations get used to doing things in certain predictable ways that work. When the environment changes, that way of doing things no longer works. But people are not accustomed to adaptation and creativity. So the business goes to the wall.

This leads us to the familiar distinction between 'management' and 'leadership'. Management is about keeping things running smoothly and efficiently. It is about all the related skills to do with organising and implementing, staffing and budgeting, keeping things on track and solving problems that arise. But it also represents a relatively narrow range of routines and an aversion to adapting.

But in times of change, it is no longer enough to keep things running well. What is required is leadership. People are needed who can envisage what a different future could be like, who can inspire others and bring them in behind the vision, who can encourage them to endure the 'pain' for the sake of the 'gain'. Strategies can be then be created for realising the vision. And that is the start of planning.

Further, that kind of planning is not a once-off. Change is not going to go away. Therefore planning is more than a momentary tactic. It is a way of thinking, a mindset. We are going to need both management and leadership skills in order to manage change in an ongoing and creative way.

Strategic planning

'Strategic' planning is a military idea, coming from the Greek word for a general. It conjures up the image of a battle where the general sees that moving his troops in such a way will make the decisive impact on the enemy and leave him victorious. This image brings us to the heart of planning. It is about the key steps that will make all the difference.

Ascertaining what these steps are arises out of a combination of a very focused idea of what you want and a quite precise idea of where you stand. It is actually something that goes on (or should be going on) all the time in our personal lives. For instance, somebody decides that they seriously need to engage in physical exercise. Somebody else sees that some kind of assertiveness training will make all the difference to them. Or a couple pinpoint that creating quality time for themselves will do more than anything else to transform their family life.

This is the dynamic. We have a sense of where we are. We have a sense of where we want to be. The real; the ideal; the gap. We find out for ourselves what are the key things that, if they were accomplished, would make a really big difference to everything else that we do. It is such a hopeful dynamic. When we 'plan' in this sense, though we do not use the word, we are asserting possibility over fatalism. We are saying that the future is not inevitable, but that we have a say in what we are going to be.

The planning process

The following is a schema of the main elements in planning:

WHERE WE ARE

WHERE WE WANT TO BE

FOCUS FOR ACTION

INITIATIVES

EVALUATION

The first two tasks are to define our current state and to define our desired state. Defining our current state is about building up an accurate and informed picture of where we actually are as a parish. The picture will include both strengths and needs, achievements and shortcomings. It will also include some consideration of the likely scenarios to unfold over the coming years – for instance, concerning demography or building projects or personnel changes.

Defining our ideal situation is about a fundamental statement of how we understand ourselves, what we are about and what we aspire to be. This is usually formulated in a 'mission statement' and/or a 'vision statement'. This is the subject of the next chapter. This vision is not all in the future. It is already being realised to some degree, so that planning is not about starting from scratch. It is incremental, building on what is there.

Planning builds on what is there already by identifying a 'focus for action'. This is the heart of the process. A focus for action makes the vision statement (which tends to be quite overarching) more specific, in light of the current and projected reality. To identify a focus for action for, say, the next few years, is to identify that which, if we were to address it successfully, would make a critical difference to our whole parish. It is to identify that which will be the focus of effort and energy, time and resources for the foreseeable future.

When the focus is agreed, detailed planning can begin. This is the 'roadmap' of how to get there. It might include a specific focus for each year, together with a more detailed programme of action for the first year. When evaluation is built in, plans can be adapted 'as we go' – things, after all, rarely go exactly according to plan. But evaluation also lets us see how, in modest ways, the 'current reality' is already being changed in the direction of the 'desired reality'

Short-circuiting
The above may look formal, yet it is a natural pattern. It is the

same as what is going on in the examples I gave above from our personal lives. But even though it makes sense it does not always happen.

What often happens is that the process is short-circuited. A group is formed, they want to justify their existence and do something. So they do something. And then they do something else. No defining the current situation, no visioning, no identifying a focus for action, and no evaluation either. The things that get done may be useful things, but there is less likelihood that they are the strategically right things to do – the things that will making a crucial difference.

It is the same in personal life. A lot of the time we drift. We fail to attend to where we are at. We neglect to dream about what we want to be. But dissatisfaction and desire are there none the less. They express themselves in our doing this and that – half-thought-out and sporadic efforts to change, that may occasionally hit the mark, but no more.

Having a plan means that the parish can stay focused on the bigger picture. There is a shared mental map. Particular initiatives are part of an overall pattern; there is a confidence about where they fit into a larger scheme of things. There is none of the frustration of doing things without any real sense of where it is all going.

Planning in scripture

The language of strategic planning is new and yet the dynamic is to be observed in our scriptures. First of all, Paul planned. It would seem that his three great missionary journeys were carefully thought-out strategies. He would focus his evangelising on a key centre in a province. Before moving on he would have established a foundation there, including a team who would bring the gospel to the outlying areas. He was 'professing' the gospel and there was something quite 'professional' about his approach.

Planning also figures significantly in the ministry of Jesus. First of all, he imagines discipleship in terms of planning. Think of the story of the man building the tower and running out of material (Luke 14), or of the foolish bridesmaids who fail to bring enough oil for their lamps (Matthew 25). The stories are about discipleship. To be a disciple is to plan, to 'count the cost'. There is a calculation involved.

Jesus planned his own life too. His time in the desert was a time for basic choices or life decisions. His choosing of the twelve and of the seventy-two were strategic decisions as to how to forward his mission. His praying before choosing the twelve (Luke 6:12) suggests a spiritual quality to his planning. The fact that the twelve stand for the twelve tribes of Israel suggests that planning is also a symbolic activity. Symbolism also characterises a final strategic decision, that embodied in Jesus' entry into Jerusalem.

God's plan

This brings us to the heart of what planning means in the faith community. What Paul does, even what Jesus does, is not adequately understood until seen as part of the magnificent enterprise that is God's plan. 'He has made known to us the mystery of his will, according to his good pleasure that he set forth in Christ, as a plan for the fullness of time' (Ephesians 1:9-10).

Thus we talk about the 'plan of salvation'. From the beginning of creation God has had in mind God's total self-communication in Christ. God has had a vision. We tend to use the word 'kingdom' as shorthand for that vision today. And this vision has been fuelled by passion. God's planning is more than the rational planning we are familiar with today. Its heart is the passion that we behold on the cross.

This impacts hugely on our Christian idea of planning. Planning is about mission and mission means God's mission. Long long before there were any 'foreign missions' we spoke of the mission emanating from God, in the Son and the Spirit, reaching out into the world with a passion and a dream.

The great changes that we are seeking to manage in our church today have brought this great grace. They have helped us connect with a sense of mission that in our complacency we had lost. This means that 'planning' in the faith community goes deeper than 'managing change'. It is an expression of a sense of mission, a new awareness of ourselves participating in God's own mission in the world.

A spirituality of planning

It is remarkable that God has chosen to pursue this mission by way of partnership with humanity. In God's plan we are not a 'provided for' humanity. We are an 'engaged with' humanity, invited to be co-creators. That is what God's momentous (strategic) decision to create freedom means. God could have made a neat, sanitised world with no pain, no suffering, no wrongdoing – and no freedom. Instead, God chose the far messier path of inviting us into partnership as co-creators, with all the attendant risks.

The same spirit is again manifest at Pentecost. Jesus 'lets go' and entrusts us with the continuance of his mission. While some think that Jesus left detailed instructions on running a church, the truth is that Jesus left it to us to carry his movement forward. Well, not entirely to us, but to us 'in the power of the Spirit'. The story of salvation is to be a partnership of the human and the divine. In God's plan we are not just acted upon; we are also on the board of directors!

This makes planning a spirituality and not just a strategy. By 'spirituality' I mean something that reaches into God. Our deepest understanding of planning is that it is what God is doing and that it is our collaboration in what God is doing. It is a divine activity that we are engaged in.

So planning is an exercise of *discernment* as well as of pure human rationality. It is done in the sense of the book of Revelation, 'Let anyone who has an ear to hear listen to what the Spirit is saying to the churches' (2:11). In thinking hard with a heart of faith, we are connecting with the movement of the Spirit in our midst, with God's amazing and unceasing creativity.

This requires a quality of contemplation. The language of

'strategic planning' can feel quite hard-nosed, but in the context of a faith community it is very different.

> 'A woman named Martha welcomed him into her home. She had a sister named Mary, who sat at the Lord's feet and listened to what he was saying. But Martha was distracted by her many tasks.' (Luke 10:38-40)

Our planning will, we trust, produce results. There will be many tasks. There will be researching and analysing, goal-setting and implementing. But at its heart there will be prayer, listening, contemplation.

At the last Supper, Thomas says to Jesus, 'Lord, we do not know where you are going; how can we know the way?' (John 14:5). Subtly, imperceptibly, we alter one word, to say, 'Lord, we do not know where *we* are going ...' That changes everything. Contemplation keeps our planning focused on asking the Lord, like Thomas, where are *you* going?

CHAPTER 8

Composing a Vision Statement

There is a saying, 'Where attention goes, energy flows.' That which grasps our attention captures our energy. We have energy for something that grasps our attention and captures our imagination. When we have a goal that we feel passionate about, all our energies conspire to work for its attainment. Without a goal we lack focus and lose energy.

Think of personal life. One person says, 'If I can save so much money a week, I will actually be able to go on that trip.' Another says, 'I'm going to do everything I possibly can to make that person happy.' And another, 'By the end of the summer, this garden is going to be transformed.' There is a goal, a dream, and there is passion about it. The energy comes flowing in, as if a dam were opened.

Underlying all such specific goals, there is the deep-seated goal of our life. It is much harder to put into words. It does not have a completion date other than death itself, because it is a goal that we are forever striving after. Exercises have been suggested, such as writing your own obituary or listening to the eulogy at your own funeral, to help put into words your life's aim.

A parish vision statement is like that. It puts into words what the parish is all about, what it is and what it strives to be. It can be concretised in specific time-scaled objectives, but it itself is dynamic, something that the parish is always on the way to, never finished reaching for.

It all depends, though, on how well it is composed and how well it is used. Many have been a waste of energy. But if it is done with care, it will have depth and power to inspire people, to align them with the vision, to motivate and energise them to be eagerly involved in its realisation.

Vision Statements and Mission Statements
The two terms, 'Vision Statement' and 'Mission Statement' have different meanings, but in a parish context they are usually used quite loosely and interchangeably. Without getting bogged down in definitions, it is worth considering the distinction briefly.

A Mission Statement has three parts. First, there is a statement of the purpose of the particular body – why do we exist? Secondly, there is a statement of the kind of business we are in, whereby we achieve our purpose. Thirdly, there is a statement of the values that guide and inspire our work.

A Vision Statement is simpler. It has been described as an artist's depiction (in words) of what the parish would look like when the mission is being accomplished. It presents the mission statement in the form of an appealing picture of what the future could look like.

What both have in common is the effort to formulate what the distinctive contribution of the parish is. In the competitive world, a mission statement seeks to get to the core of the distinctive competency of this particular business or organisation, that which gives it its competitive edge. In our context this translates into getting to the core of what our parish is all about, its core contribution to people's lives, what it offers that is original and unique.

There is much, for instance, that the parish has in common with community development work, but that is not what is distinctive to parish. The question might be formulated as follows: *'What is it, above all else, that the parish can offer to people today?'*

Illustrations
The following, from the parish of the Holy Redeemer, Bray, is a good example of a mission statement. An overarching statement of purpose is followed by bulleted points describing how the

purpose is to be achieved, and this is followed by a statement of values;

> 'Our Christian community of the parish of the Holy Redeemer is dedicated to serving the Kingdom of God through...
> - the provision of social and support services and material facilities;
> - bringing people closer to God through nourishment of the spirit and development of faith, recognising the Eucharist as the source and summit of Christian life;
> - bearing witness to Christian values;
> - openness to change and commitment to ongoing renewal;
> - commitment to reach out to those who, for whatever reason, do not feel they belong in our community;
> - commitment to an all-inclusive community where everyone is equal, welcome and valued, with a sense of belonging.
>
> We strive to achieve this by using the gifts and talents in our community, through a spirit of partnership between the laity and clergy.'

The following, from the parish of Greystones, has similarities, but is more in the form of a vision statement:

> 'We the parishioners of Holy Rosary and Saint Kilian desire to become a parish where caring for one another in the way Jesus taught us will be recognised as the basis for everything else we do.'

Focusing sharply

These illustrations also show how vision and mission run into one another and there is no point being pedantic about it. Maybe the thing to aim for is the key central statement. People can then decide how much elaboration they wish to add.

It is worth asking, what is the desirable length of the statement? A strong succinct statement has great power to align people behind the vision. At the same time, Martin Luther King's 'I have a dream' was a speech! But a longer statement can dilute the power. It can also be a kind of lowest common denominator, because it is trying to please everybody or include a reference to everybody's hobby-horse.

Mission statements, while longer, make a helpful differentiation between the purpose of the parish and the business of the parish – the end and the means. For example, is a sense of welcome and belonging the means or the end? Is vibrant liturgy the means or the end? Is evangelisation the means or the end? The distinction forces people to clarify sharply what they are ultimately about and to distinguish that from how they are going about it.

The point is that the 'how' can change. For instance, an organisation that is focused on love for the poor may change its approach, from distributing charitable donations to providing education and counselling services. But sometimes people can confuse the 'how' with the mission. They are imprisoned by thinking 'this is the way we have always done it' and they are losing touch with the vision.

Guiding questions

There is a choice of different questions that can be used to evoke the kind of responses that will feed into a statement of vision or mission. The following are some examples:

What is the purpose of the church?

What is our parish for?

'Ideally, our parish is a place where…'

(complete the sentence).

'Our parish should be "parish of the year" because…'

(complete the sentence).

'The mission of the parish, as I see it, is…'

(complete the sentence).

A choice from questions such as the following could add a local flavour, by focusing on the specific traits of this particular parish:

How would you describe the spirit of this parish?

What do you find life-giving about this parish?

What attracts you to want to belong to this parish?

What do you most value about this parish?

What is the biggest impact this parish has made on your life?

How to go about it

Ownership is key to a successful vision statement. If a small group gets together and engages in an exercise to produce a vision, the exercise may prove quite enriching for themselves, but it may go no further than that. When they bring the statement of vision to the parish, others may legitimately ask, *'whose vision?'* The vision will only really be powerful for those who feel that it is *theirs*. If it is to be the parish's vision, the parish as a whole needs to be consulted.

At the same time there is an art in composing a vision statement. Some people have the gift of being able to gather what people are saying and to formulate it in a way that is not only accurate but inspiring. So, while the consultation should be wide, there needs to be a small editing or writing team to make the most of the feedback.

Remember that the exercise itself is nearly as important as the outcome. When people are engaged in articulating their own identity and vision, they are engaged in a process that is formative. They are deepening their own sense of parish, of faith, of kingdom, of each other. They are growing as a faith community. If the exercise is seen simply as a means to an end, it may lose out on being this kind of experience.

One way of going about it would be for a group such as the pastoral council to produce a draft statement. The group would spend some time reflecting on what parish is all about. They would spend time reflecting on the richness of their parish's life. They would try to formulate all this in a statement that would seek to 'mirror' the parish to itself. A feedback and redrafting process would follow.

Alternatively, the group could go to the parish with nothing prepared, lest it constrain people's thinking. They would give a

clear explanation of what is sought and this would be accompanied by a great deal of marketing and motivating. Responses
could be sought at parish meetings or from the parish groups or
on the website and so on. Eventually a draft would be returned
to the parish for comment and revision.

This might all seem very complicated, but it is the only way
that is worth it. If the vision statement is to be an enduring and
inspiring source of mission for the faith-community, then it
must needs be a fairly extensive and protracted process. Less of
an investment will only produce a correspondingly less satisfying result. It is not unlike the difference between an inspiring
and a pedestrian homily!

Keeping the vision alive
There are a lot of vision statements lying in drawers or fading on
notice-boards. Quite an amount of energy went into the composition. But when it was completed it was as if the process ran out
of fuel and was just left there.

The whole point of a vision statement is that people keep it
before them. I am reminded of the words of Moses to Israel:

> You shall love the Lord your God with all your heart and
> with all your soul and with all your might. Keep these words
> that I am commanding you today in your heart. Recite them
> to your children and talk about them when you are at home
> and when you are away, when you lie down and when you
> rise. Bind them as a sign on your hand, fix them as an em-
> blem on your forehead and write them on the doorposts of
> your house and on your gates. (Deuteronomy 6:5-9)

A vision statement – be it that of an individual or that of a faith
community – is something that we carry everywhere. It is part of
us. It informs all that we do. It is a constant point of reference
and a constant source of challenge. 'Where attention goes, energy
flows.'

A first step would be to launch the vision statement. Make it
the occasion of celebration. For instance, build the weekend
liturgies around it, including a formal 'unveiling' with attendant

expressions of thanks and hope. Produce an attractive card for all to bring home, with the vision statement and an accompanying prayer. In this way the parish as a whole is being drawn in again and focused on its own essential nature.

After that, the focus can be kept up in various ways. Parish groups might be asked to incorporate it into their every prayer. Notes of meetings might include it at the top of the page. It might occasionally be incorporated into the prayers of the faithful and the homily. It might be displayed prominently on the website, the newsletter, the notice-boards. Whatever way, it has to be kept alive. A vision statement is not capable of independent survival outside the hearts of parishioners!

Using the vision statement

Since the vision statement of its nature is quite general, it also needs to be concretised so as to generate action. One way of doing this is to set short-to-medium-term goals. Using the vision statement as the backdrop – and taking into account likely scenarios regarding demography, building projects, personnel changes and so on – the parish would formulate an inspiring goal for, say, the next three to five years.

John F. Kennedy said, 'By the end of the decade, a man on the moon.' It would be hard to formulate anything quite so focused, but the potential is clear. In one diocese 'reaching out' was chosen as the key focus for the coming years. It is easy to understand. People can identify with it. It relates to a felt need. It motivates. It is capable of application in a whole range of pastoral initiatives. In one parish 'taking responsibility for our own future' was taken as the goal for the next five years. Again it is a focus that has the potential to unite and to galvanise.

Another way is to agree on a theme for the coming year. Again using the vision statement as a backdrop, the parish would take on a theme that is strongly reflective of the vision and very inspirational in itself. In one parish the theme of 'welcome and belonging' was identified as the key focus for the year, with quite significant outcomes.

There is something inspirational about such a choice. It is simple and it is profound. It captures something of the soul of what parish is all about. It is easy to see how it could focus energy. It is easy to see how it could be broken down – for instance, into different areas of activity, such as liturgy or hospitality, or into different populations, such as young people or housebound people.

No vision statement, short of the gospel proclamation itself, will last for ever. If it has been developed with care it will produce fruit for a number of years. It will last longer if it is returned to in prayer, to allow its riches to reveal themselves anew. But there will be a time for review, where the faith community would be asked to comment in the light of their experience since it was first produced. That, hopefully, would be the opportunity for the life of the parish to enter a new phase.

CHAPTER 9

Parishes Together

In recent times there has been a growing interest in the together-ness of parishes, in how they might be together and do together in a new way. Some have already travelled a good way down this road; others are coming to grips with the idea; others again feel that they have enough on their plate already! But it is emerging more and more clearly that this is the way forward.

The reason why it is the way forward may not, however, be so clear. The most obvious reason why is the pragmatic one. With less and less clergy we no longer expect that there will be a priest in each parish. It is only a few decades ago in expanding urban areas that new parishes were being constituted, almost in a form of cell multiplication. Now it looks as if the process is contracting and bigger units comprising a small number of neighbouring parishes is the prospect before us.

But this is not the deep reason for the togetherness of parishes. It is more the occasion for collaboration than the heart of it. Partnership between parishes is not at heart an emergency response to a reduction in clergy. It is something that is right in itself. It is in fact another feature of what a parish is and is meant to be. We need to reflect on this first, before looking at any of the practicalities.

Partnership in ministry
'Collaboration' means 'working with'. So, who is it that is working with whom? Our first answer would probably be that the collaboration is between clergy and laity. While that is crucial, it is only the start. When we reflect further, we find that the answer is much longer than we supposed.

Much of the challenge of partnership is not about priests and laity working together. It is about priests learning to work with one another! Today priests are learning to work with one another in a new way, leaving behind the individualistic 'lone ranger' style of ministry of the past.

Lay people too are learning to be with each other in a new way. They are learning to cherish each other's gifts. They are leaving behind the attitude of 'who do they think they are', as they realise that we are all called to be co-responsible. Ultimately this calls for a parish-wide sense of ownership where all are truly responsible for all.

Priests and religious too are challenged to learn partnership with one another. Those in religious life bring different perspectives, approaches and emphases to parish ministry. It is a gift to the parish that has not always been fully appreciated or integrated.

The emergence of lay pastoral workers creates new possibilities and challenges for partnership. This time it is a call to collaboration between the 'professionals' in ministry, be they lay, religious or ordained. It is also a call to think out anew the partnership between paid and voluntary ministry.

Collaboration also means a new quality of networking and cohesion between different groups in the parish. It invites us to develop new forms of partnership between school, home and parish, particularly in the context of sacramental preparation. On another front, it invites different Eucharistic communities within the same parish to consider their alliance.

Within all this there are more subtle challenges, in the parish and beyond. There is the challenge to a real equality of men and women. There is the challenge to a real solidarity of rich and poor. These dimensions of partnership echo Paul's radical words to the Galatians: 'There is no longer Jew or Greek, there is no longer slave or free, there is no longer male or female; for all of you are one in Christ Jesus' (Galatians 3:28).

Looking outward, collaborative ministry draws parishes together, the subject of this chapter. It may be the grouping of neighbouring parishes. It may be twinning with a parish from the developing world or with a parish nearer to hand in more straitened circumstances.

Inter-parish partnership reaches further to invite a new quality of partnership across the diocese as a whole and between the bishop and the diocese. More and more we are learning to see that the diocese is the key unit in developing pastoral strategies for the future. Beyond that again, dioceses can pool together the wisdom from their experience in negotiating today's new challenges.

Collaborative ministry also stretches out towards other churches and beliefs. There are possibilities emerging at parish level for the different Christian churches to become partners in ministry. And, as our society becomes multicultural, there is now an inter-faith as well as an inter-church dimension to collaboration in the parish.

Finally, partnership reaches beyond a religious context. 'Parish' and 'community', which were once synonymous, are now called to new forms of alliance. Rather than see itself as an oasis in a hostile world, the faith community can learn to appreciate how it shares with others of different beliefs a common conviction about and commitment to the dignity of the human person.

A truth

All this is saying very impressively that collaborative ministry is a whole new culture. It is not something that comes and goes, like the parish sodality for instance. It is a whole new way of being church. One of the guiding insights of today's church is that ministry is of its nature collaborative, that partnership is at the heart of what we are meant to be as church.

Partnership is a truth about church. The reason why is because it is a truth about God. Partnership, simply, is God's way with humanity. In creating the world, God established us as co-creators. In the Pentecost gift of the Spirit, Jesus made us partners in the divine mission. Awesome as it sounds, the way God has chosen is that we would be co-responsible for the plan of salvation.

Part of what we mean by 'Trinity' is that this spirit reaches into God's self. God's own life is an unspeakably dynamic interweaving of life and love, unity and diversity. And what is the heart of God must needs be the heart of the church. We have no option about a spirituality of partnership. It is of God.

In this light, 'collaboration' appears a rather bland term. I am led to prefer the corresponding Greek root, 'synergy'. It too translates as 'working together', but in contemporary English usage it has the further connotation of an energy released in our relating together. This energy is the Holy Spirit.

A triple structure
Parishes together is simply one important aspect of this deeper and pervasive truth. I would suggest that parishes look on partnership structures as having three layers

There is, first of all, the parish leadership group, pastoral council, whatever it is called. That structure is not just functional. It is also symbolic, its presence a statement that collaborative ministry is about all of us becoming really responsible for all.

Secondly, there is partnership between parishes. One expression of this is team ministry between neighbouring parishes. This will come to supersede the traditional deanery or vicariate structures, which were exclusively clerical and in many cases too large for the kind of collaboration envisaged today.

Another expression is what we call twinning. Usually twinning is international, a solidarity with a parish from the developing world, with all the mutual enrichment it brings. But it is also more local, where the parish's gratitude for its own resources becomes an imperative to share resources with another parish not so fortunate.

Thirdly, there is diocese-wide partnership, where the creativity at parish and inter-parish levels are part of a bigger picture. Partnership at this level may be expressed in a diocesan pastoral plan and in some form of diocesan pastoral council, driving the whole project of partnership. In that scenario there is ideally a combination of a strong sense of local ownership with committed diocesan leadership and resourcing.

Thinking differently
It is arresting that the adjective of the word parish – 'parochial' – means being limited, narrow, insular in outlook. Our tradition has been one where parishes existed in a kind of 'splendid isolation', each a kingdom onto itself. The old canon law saw the parish as more or less the property of the parish priest. Priests had to get permission to enter each other's territory for any exercise of ministry.

Today we have begun to think differently. We are moving towards seeing the local grouping of neighbouring parishes – perhaps three or four or five – as the unit. Instead of having a priest in each parish, we may have three or four priests, possibly living together, ministering as a team to a group of parishes. Just as currently many parishes are comprised of two or more Eucharistic communities, so in the future there will be a new inter-parish unit comprised of a number of our current parishes. It has already begun.

People, though, will still identify with their parish. Autonomy will not be lost. There will be a leadership team in each parish. The local feel will not be swallowed up. The Gaelic Athletic Association provides an analogy in the structure of club and county. There can be a strong sense of identification and participation at both levels. Tensions will need to be addressed, but always as a matter of 'both-and', never 'either-or'.

An original idea
Parishes together, while new and unfamiliar to us, goes back to our origins as church, to the first few decades in fact. There we find Paul encouraging the Christians in Macedonia and Achaia in organising a collection for the relief of the Christians in Jerusalem. The phrase 'God loves a cheerful giver' (2 Corinthians 9:7) comes from the passage where he is reflecting on the sense of generosity and solidarity demonstrated.

At a time when 'church' meant the local faith community, this initiative was an important step in developing collaboration between these communities and in developing a sense of 'church' itself as a communion of communities. Paul's words about the Body of Christ are apt for this context, 'If one member suffers, all suffer together with it; if one member is honoured, all rejoice together with it' (1 Corinthians 12:26).

The truth is that 'parish' cannot be understood in isolation. Parish can only be fully itself in relationships of peace and solidarity with fellow faith communities, those that are neighbouring and those that are needy. Of its nature parish is meant to be drawn outwards and looking outwards. Part of the role of the bishop in the diocese is to be a symbol of this by encouraging parishes to be interested in one another, to network and to develop solidarity.

The possibilities

Partnership between parishes (thinking now of those in geographical proximity) can be anywhere on a scale from minimal to maximal. It can simply be an occasional affair of the priests meeting together, or assisting each other with Masses in summer or communal Services of Reconciliation. At the other end of the scale, neighbouring parishes can decide to view themselves as a unit, with the priests and pastoral workers forming a single team.

The thrust in our time is from the former to the latter. This can be seen where priests take time out together for reflection and renewal. It can be seen where neighbouring parishes sit down to discuss together the future scenario regarding the number of priests and the number of Masses in the area. Parochialism and splendid isolation are giving way to the strength that comes from togetherness.

The more parishes are together, the more the possibilities expand. Groups from the different parishes can meet to encourage one another, share ideas and organise joint training programmes. In some ministries the area can be treated as a unit – for instance,

a joint course for sacramental preparation, or a single bereavement team, or a parish mission for the whole area. Common
policies can be worked out, for instance around funeral practices
or the reception of those seeking Christian marriage or baptism.

In a time of mobility, where people choose where to worship,
parishes together can achieve a standard of quality and excel-
lence across the whole area. Together they can generate a creative and effective 'new evangelisation', capable of connecting
the good news of the gospel with the experience of people
today. As part of this, parishes together may be able to engage a
paid pastoral worker or liturgist or youth minister.

With parishes together, each Eucharistic community can be
confident about its future A team of priests will be responsible
for the area as a whole, rotating among the different churches
for Masses and services. Even the *Aifreann Gaeilge*, one of the
first casualties of reduced clergy, can be confident of survival
when it is parishes together that care for it.

The theme of twinning is worth mentioning here again. Even
when neighbouring parishes learn to work together, there is still
the possibility of parochialism, just that now the unit is larger!
Twinning stands as a constant reminder that we must strive
beyond complacency in our parish units. Parishes must ever re-
mind themselves of the manner in which their 'centre of gravity'
lies beyond themselves. Parish is not fully parish until it feels
called to solidarity by the greater needs of other faith communities near and far.

The benefits
Many of the further benefits have already been alluded to. The
benefits of sharing talents and pooling resources. The benefits of
support and encouragement, especially for groups struggling
on their own and for priests working in isolation. The enrichment of diversity, the learning from one another's experience.

Parishes together means 'synergy'. Instead of the experience
of pressure there will be an experience of energy released, just
the energy that was needed. Instead of the feeling of a slow,

continuing decline, there will be a feeling of hope, a sense that we are proactively contending with the challenges. Instead of the deadening confines of parochialism there will be the liberating experience of a wider church. Instead of more clericalism, it will be a people's church.

As in every healthy relationship, being together will enhance identity. Difference and autonomy will not be smothered, as is sometimes feared. A genuine relationship is one where you become more yourself, not less. This suggests that the way to begin is with a focus on relationships rather than structures. If we begin by getting to know one another and learning to trust each other, the structures will evolve to reflect our growing togetherness.

CHAPTER 10

Getting People Involved

Something a friend of mine said once taught me a lot about this topic. He said that when you add up all the people who are involved in the parish, you should add in also the family members who mind the children while those people are out working for the parish. Besides the person who is involved there is the person who is facilitating that involvement. Both are *equally* involved.

'How to get people involved' is a regularly expressed concern in parishes (though the concern is not confined to parishes). It deserves serious reflection. But, as the above illustrates, there is a lot more to it than meets the eye. When we unpack 'what is involved in being involved', we find that there is a lot to be hopeful about.

Getting involved and feeling involved

I think the place to start is with that word 'involvement'. I would propose a fundamental distinction between people 'getting involved' and people 'feeling involved'. In many ways this is the key to the whole question.

Think, for example, of people at Mass on Sunday. There is a choir, there is the priest, there are ministers of the Word and of the Eucharist, there are the servers, ushers perhaps, the collectors … and there is the congregation. Who is 'involved'?

We might be inclined to say that those who are doing things are the most involved. Not necessarily. After all, people's minds can be a hundred miles away from what they are doing! The person most 'involved' might well be the person sitting down the church, 'doing' nothing, but participating intensely, listening to the scripture, bringing their concerns to the altar, feeling at home, going away refreshed and challenged.

What matters most is that people *feel* involved. If people feel involved, then they are involved, often in a very profound way. Involvement is about people having a sense of welcome and belonging. It is about them hearing in the parish the message, 'we notice you; we care that you exist'. It is about a faith community that gives people a sense of God in their lives. It is about people identifying with this faith community.

'Getting involved' is a narrower idea. It has to do with specific ministries and groups in the parish. Generally people who feel involved will be more disposed to getting involved in that sense. It also happens that 'getting involved' in something is what makes a person 'feel involved'. But overall, feeling involved is the central idea. At any point in time only some people will be involved in specific ways. But everybody can and should feel involved.

Affirmation

People feel involved when there is a sense of welcome in the parish and when everything that is done is permeated with a feeling of welcome. But a major part of welcome is about noticing people. It is about a sense of appreciation for people and for what goes on in their lives.

Another way of putting this is to say that very many people are already involved without realising it! They live lives that are inspired by kingdom values. In their love for their family, in their practice of integrity, in their passion for justice and peace, in the contemplation of their hearts, they are already living the gospel. But they have not made the link. I recall the woman who said to the parish priest; 'Now that I have reared my family, I'd like to do something for the church'!

One very important way in which people are already involved is where somebody is giving time to something outside the parish. They might be involved in Meals on Wheels or The Samaritans or a developing world project or cancer support.

There are hundreds of such ways in which people are living their discipleship. They are engaged in the work of God's kingdom. If parish is there for the sake of the world, then these people are involved in their parish in a very real way.

Think of that phrase we use, the 'practising Catholic'. In our equating its meaning with somebody who goes to Mass, we have disregarded other aspects – such as personal prayer, thinking of others, witnessing to Christian values, participating in the community, seeking to understand God, striving for justice and peace. There is a lot more 'practising' going on than we know of.

Involving people in the parish may be primarily about affirming the involvement that is already there. If people do not make the link, then the link needs to be made for them. People deserve to be reassured about the God who is already in their lives. They need to be encouraged to rejoice that their lives are already full of faith and hope and love.

Maybe we need to think differently. While we call the Eucharist the 'source and summit' of Christian life, we should not demote the rest of Christian life. If anything it is the other way around. The primary place where God is revealed and manifested is in the 'day-to-dayness' of life. God is in the day-to-day, in the ordinary. What happens in the Eucharist is that we heighten our awareness of the God who is there all the time.

Indeed, awareness is a big part of affirmation. A lot of the time we think in terms of making people more aware of the parish. But maybe it is the other way around. Maybe it is about the parish becoming more aware of people, of the real concerns of their lives, of the God who is already silently there. The first step in people becoming more aware of the parish is for the parish to become more aware of them.

Getting involved

If we turn to the more specific question of 'getting people involved', it is interesting how people see it differently. Some say that it is next to impossible to get people involved in the parish and that people no longer want to be involved. But others say that people are willing, it is just a matter of how to connect with them. I am inclined to think that the latter, more hopeful view may be nearer the truth.

At the same time it is clear that parishes generally are dissatisfied that few enough people are involved. It might be good to ask, therefore: what is it that prevents people from being involved? I will list a number of factors that people mention:

- Some people, particularly those with young families, find that their lives are too full and pressured to allow for any further involvement in the parish.
- Some people who are open to getting involved are frightened off by what they see before them. The 'same old faces' around for years and years makes it look as if getting involved is a life-sentence.
- Some say that the church is not inviting; it is not personal enough to attract them to get involved. This can include the feeling that some parish groups are a 'closed shop'.
- Quite a number of people lack confidence. They would like to become involved but do not think that they have anything to offer; or that they have the knowledge and skills for the work.
- There are lots of people who would have become involved long ago except nobody ever asked them!
- Some people feel that they would not be treated as equals. They might think that the priest does not regard them as being of the same standing as himself; or that getting involved would mean being used to do jobs for the priest.
- Others are put off by the reaction of their fellow parishioners, by people who say, 'Who does he think he is?' or 'Soon she'll want to run the parish'.

It is clear from this that in most parishes there are many people who would enjoy being involved, but something is preventing them – something in themselves, something in their circumstances, something in the parish.

Of course there are also people who do not want to be involved. But in many cases it may be understandable why this is so. People were brought up in a culture where 'ministry' was what the priest did, where the job of the laity was, as somebody put it, 'only to believe'. Just like the experience of 'doctor knows best', 'just do as I say'. With such a background it is no wonder that so many people see the parish as a kind of service-provider, with no sense of ownership or co-responsibility.

Clearing the way

From the above it is clear that there are a number of things to be done in order to clear the way for people to get involved. In other words, before looking at specific suggestions, there are some fundamental orientations for the parish to take in order to create a climate where people would be attracted to become involved.

Firstly, there is what was said above, namely, to put a good deal of thought and energy into affirming the grace and giftedness in people's lives. They might come to Mass and no more. They might not even do that much. Yet their lives are full of goodness and Christian living and prayer. People need to be noticed and deserve to be affirmed in the ways in which they are already involved.

Developing an atmosphere and ethos of welcome in the parish is a big part of this. All, whether they are churchgoers or on the fringes, should experience God's own welcoming heart reaching out to them in the hospitality and friendliness they experience in the parish.

Secondly, much thought and energy has to put into the shift of mindset from a clerical church to a people's church. There is a lot of educating to be done in order for people to grow into a sense of ownership, a sense that this is our parish where we are all equal and all really responsible for all. This is probably the fundamental task of parish renewal, but it is absolutely basic to people getting involved.

Many Sunday Masses illustrate this issue. There may be hundreds of people in the church. Yet there may no reader. Or there might be only one or two ministers of the Eucharist. There may be nobody singing. The 'theory' is that we are all celebrating the Eucharist together, but it does not feel like 'ours'. It is all left to the priest. The singing is left to the choir. There is a deflating sense of people passively being provided for – and consenting to it.

Thirdly, existing parish groups need to communicate a sense of welcome. These groups are the subject of a separate chapter below. But it is clear, notwithstanding the generous spirit and wonderful work of such groups, that groups can themselves be an obstacle to people getting involved. Some groups look like a closed shop. Or they can give the impression that getting involved is something that will last for decades on end.

Fourthly, the parish may need to be less demanding on its volunteers. Sometimes it asks too much of a generous co-worker, making the work unpleasant. Sometimes it can be reluctant in letting somebody go when they feel their time is done. Not alone is this unfair to the people involved; it also puts others off.

Personal contact
Personal contact is the single most effective way of involving people in parish ministries. There are many people, with some time and great gifts, who would respond gladly if there were a personal contact that made them feel wanted and reassured them about the contribution they could make.

Priests obviously have a huge role here because they have come in contact with so many people through their ministry. They can communicate a genuine sense of wanting to involve people in the life of the parish as equal co-workers. They can make it clear that they are not using people but affirming their calling and giftedness. And they can leave space for people to say 'no', given that some might find it hard to say 'no' to the priest.

But lay people have a big role too. They may need to be encouraged by the priest to appreciate that it is their right to invite fellow parishioners to become involved. Everybody knows somebody who would enjoy being involved. All they need is for a friend or neighbour to say, 'I think you would be great at that.'

People who are already involved have a role here in communicating to others the joy and fulfilment they themselves experience in parish ministry.

Making ministry attractive
The joy and fulfilment is a very important factor. Sometimes the impression can be given that parish involvement is all about giving. That is not true. Ministry is both a giving and a receiving and we are not nearly clear enough about that. When those already involved are asked how they experience their involvement, they speak about how they enjoy it, how they experience a sense of satisfaction. They speak about the friendship and the support. They talk about how their life is enriched and their faith deepened.

They talk, that is, mainly about what they receive! They also talk about giving, for instance about wanting to give something back to the church, about wanting to help others and to make a difference. But it is both a giving and a receiving. More people will be attracted to become involved if they feel that this is something that is going to enhance their lives – as opposed to some dreary chore they will never be able to get out of.

People will also be more attracted to become involved if the involvement looks both real and manageable. People need to be able to see the merit of the particular activity and to believe that it delivers something tangible and worthwhile. They also need to see that the commitment has a start, a middle and an end. It is easier to say 'yes' to a month or a year than to 'forever'.

Other initiatives
Parish visitation is another occasion for contacting people. Again, this is the subject of a separate chapter. The kind of visitation I am talking about is where teams of lay people visit the dwellings in the parish, as an expression of welcome and hospitality and perhaps to distribute information about the parish. In the course of that work they will come into contact with a variety of needs and a variety of gifts.

Providing information is a route that is often neglected. Most parishes have more going on than people realise. Even people who are already involved are often surprised when a list is made of all the parish groups and activities. It makes sense to publicise and proclaim and celebrate all that is going on, and in the process to invite people to consider if there something there for themselves. This will be taken up again in the chapter about parish ministry groups.

One final possibility, with untapped potential, is simply to bring people together. For example, if a facility is provided for parents of young children to meet each other, or for retired people to gather, people can then begin to talk about their own lives and needs. They can begin to minister to one another and to themselves. The energy here will be high because people are responding to their own felt needs. There is something in this that should characterise all efforts to get people involved, namely, that getting involved is not about somebody else's agenda, but about our own, because it is our parish and our lives.

CHAPTER 11

Ministry Groups in the Parish

The various groups that minister in the parish make an inestimable contribution to the life of the faith-community. But they have their own needs too. Supporting them has to be a high priority, a priority in particular for the parish pastoral council. There are a number of important ways in which the life of these groups can be enriched and their contribution to parish life enhanced.

The positives
Ministry is a different experience for different people and groups in the parish. The issues for ministers of the Eucharist are not the same as those facing a youth ministry group. A parish choir and a communications group have diverse questions and concerns. Alongside this variety, there are some common positives and negatives in the experience of parish ministry groups today.

On the positive side is the great enrichment they bring to parish life. Imagine parish liturgy without choirs, music groups and cantors; without ministers of the Eucharist and ministers of the Word; without the creativity of liturgy groups; without those behind the scenes in the church. Think of how care groups, visitation groups, bereavement groups and hospitality groups have deepened the experience of welcome and belonging in the community. Think of how baptism teams and funeral teams, first communion and confirmation teams create such effective outreach to people 'on the fringes'.

Also on the positive side is what the experience has meant for the people in these groups. It has meant for many a new and exciting experience of church. It has meant a new sense of vocation for both priests and people, as they work together, sharing their gifts, on ministry groups and pastoral councils. It has meant a deepening of faith and an increase of hope.

The needs

There are also some concerns that need to be tackled. We talk about the 'same old faces'. I already mentioned how groups do not always invite involvement. It may be a group that has been together for years. They are close-knit and now maybe they are growing older together. Without intending it they may have become a closed shop, even a clique. They may not want any new members. 'The same old faces' can also send out the message that getting involved is a life-sentence. People naturally try to evade capture!

In some ministries it is also possible that the work becomes more of a job or a routine than a ministry. This may be more true of ministries that do not have a strong group aspect to them. For instance, ministers of the Word and ministers of the Eucharist can slip into this pattern. Once they are trained in, there may not be much more attention paid to them and their work can become devoid of preparation and of depth.

Groups, too, can be disconnected. Each group is taking care of its own patch and may be doing so very well. There may be little or no communication or co-ordination with other groups. Efforts may be duplicated; information may never get through. Worse, there can be a strongly asserted sense of territoriality, making one wonder, whose needs are being served here?

Finally, there is a concern that transcends any particular group. The parish may have a great variety of flourishing ministry groups. It can be easy to conclude that, because there is so much going on, all the needs are basically being met. But rarely, if ever, is there such a neat match between what is being done and what needs to be done. There are real, felt needs out there that our very success may prevent us from seeing.

What are parish groups for?

All of this, the positives and the concerns, confirms the importance of taking parish ministry groups seriously. But before
going any further I would like to reflect on the fundamental purpose of these groups.

'Purposes,' you might say; surely each group has a different
purpose? The finance group are doing one thing, the justice and
peace group something else. That is true, but underlying those
different functions and purposes is a common aim that in fact is
the heart of each group's work. Generally speaking, this aim is
dormant in the consciousness of groups themselves, as their attention is absorbed by the task in hand.

The underlying aim of each parish ministry group is to enable or activate the ministry of all God's people. The goal of the
baptism team is that the baptismal call would come alive in people. The goal of the ministers of the Word is that people would
make the connections between their lives and the Word of life.
The goal of the ministers of the Eucharist is that people realise
that we all are the Body of Christ. The goal of the choir and cantors is that all of our lives would be a living song of praise to the
Lord. The goal of the care and bereavement groups is that suffering and death would mark a further deepening in our experience of discipleship.

Each group is there to serve. But service is more than providing a service. That could too easily perpetuate the hold on people of a 'provided-for' church where ministry is something that
other people do 'for me'. Rather, service means being at the service of the baptism call of all, to understand that they are loved
by God and called to love in turn. The work of the groups is
done, not when a task has been completed, but when God's people are experiencing themselves as a ministering community.

This perspective is crucial. A multitude of active ministry
groups could give a false impression. Even though there might
be many people 'involved', they remain a small fraction of the
faith community. It is only when there is a widespread sense of
'feeling involved' that things are going really well. It is only

when the faith community as a whole is moving from being 'provided for' to being a ministering community that the parish is really alive.

This has to become the goal and focus of each group in the parish. In this context we can go on to look at some of the ways in which parish groups can be enabled in their aim. In the suggestions that follow, the parish pastoral council has the key role, for it is its distinctive role to make these things happen.

Encouragement

There was a bishop who would only comment on priests' work if there was something wrong; if he said nothing, they could presume they were doing alright. Many leaders are like that. As a result, many people in ministry, priests as much as anybody else, can go for long periods of time with hardly any affirmation at all. That can gradually deaden the spirit.

A first imperative, therefore, is to pay attention to parish groups. Many people are giving many hours of their best effort. It is greatly important for the parish leadership to pay attention, to acknowledge, to appreciate, to affirm, to 'care for the carers'. There is no describing what this attention can mean to people in ministry. We all brighten up when we are noticed!

As I said, the pastoral council has a key role. It aims to create a relationship with all the groups in the parish. Perhaps through some kind of liaison system, members of the council connect with different groups, respectful of their autonomy, to express interest, to invite feedback, to offer support if desired.

This might be a stepping stone to further encouragement. For instance, the council might work on ways to communicate with the parish about all that is being done by the groups. Here I am thinking of the good that can be done simply by proclaiming all that is going on in the parish. In most parishes people do not realise the half of it. When they do they can be enormously appreciative.

I am thinking of one parish where they went with the image of the vine and the branches. Right along one wall of the church they arranged a long (artificial) vine, the branches decorated with large print descriptions and photos of the different parish groups, and the parish vision statement at the centre. Besides being a revelation to parishioners, it was a boost to the people in the various groups.

Enrichment

The experience of ministry is itself an enrichment, but this needs to be complemented and enhanced by providing enrichment in more specific ways. Many groups begin their life with some form of training or initiation, which can be quite formative. But after that it is down to work. Further opportunities for refreshment and renewal can be rare. It often happens that a group's conversation about parish and ministry never goes further than the task in hand.

Enrichment sessions could focus on generating a renewed sense of the role of the group. Groups can be helped to appreciate the deeper significance of their work. In and through their own specific role, they are also helping to bring into being a truly ministering community. What this means deserves to be teased out. The kind of vision that emerges can inspire and energise the group, as well as affirming them in what they are doing.

Enrichment sessions can also bring the group to a deeper appreciation of their particular area of ministry. For instance, ministers of the Word might reflect on how scripture has been becoming more and more central to the faith experience since Vatican II. A communications group might reflect on the way in which communication is the heart of God's revelation in Christ and the heart of building Christian community.

Again, a justice and peace group might reflect on the new scripture-inspired vision of justice that has taken hold of the church since the advent of liberation theology. Or the ministers of the Eucharist might reflect on the richness of meanings contained in the phrase, 'the Body of Christ'. In each case the group is being affirmed in the profound theological meaning of what they do.

Enrichment can also have an element of evaluation and re-training. It is an opportunity to weed out bad practices and to name good practice. It is an opportunity too to look at how the organisation of this particular ministry could be made more effective. In all of this the group is learning a more proactive ownership of its ministry.

Networking
It seems to be a pattern in parishes that ministry groups are like the spokes of a wheel. Each group is connected in to the priest, who alone has an overall picture of what is going on. There is little interaction between the groups themselves. Each is absorbed in its own area of work. They may have little or no familiarity with the work and concerns of one another. They might not know the people in the other groups.

Notwithstanding the good work being done, there is an isolation and a separateness here that is unsatisfactory. In the end it means that there is a lack of explicit overall cohesion in the work of the parish as a whole. Networking can tap the potential that lies dormant in this situation.

The first thing is for people to get to know each other. A parish open day, with displays from the different groups is a great chance for people from the different groups to meet. That on its own can be a great lift for everybody, especially becoming aware that they are part of something bigger than just their own group. This is at least as valuable as the number of new recruits that such a day may throw up.

Meeting together in clusters can be a springboard for mutual collaboration. There might be a few groups who are in the general area of caring ministries. There are others who are all involved in music ministry. These sets of groups can begin to network, to dream together, to share resources, to streamline their operation.

Ultimately networking can lead to common vision. As groups communicate with one another, hopefully any sense of territoriality will be dissipated. Groups can be initiated into an inspiring sense of the vision of parish that they all share. As the parish enters into a planning mode, each group can see how its effort fits into an overall scheme, like the parts of the body in St Paul's image, each of them vital in its own distinctive way.

Recruiting

Perhaps the first need that most groups will express is about getting new members. In this area the pastoral council can offer both a support and a challenge.

On the support side, the key contribution of the council is its focusing the parish on the goal of becoming a ministering community with a pervasive sense of 'feeling involved'. It can also help in more specific ways – for instance, organising a parish day as mentioned above, or a 'Ministering Sunday' where there is an invitation from the altar to join specified groups. There are always people who are waiting to be asked. At the same time, personal one-to-one contact remains the most effective way of recruiting. The pastoral council might keep reminding the groups of that.

On the challenge side, groups need to consider just how welcoming they are. Often that is where the problem lies. If a new member joins, that means it is a new group for everybody. If the existing group is a tight-knit closed shop, will they be up to that challenge? Maybe they do not really want any newcomers, in which case there is no room for complaint and they can be left to grow old gracefully.

Welcome also means rollover of membership. If people see that parish groups have an exit as well as an entry they will be less fearful of joining. They will be more attracted if they see that there is a constant turnover, where people give a certain time commitment and then move on.

Parishes have a poor record here, too intent on holding on to people instead of constantly looking out for new faces. It should almost be a principle that people have to move on. In that way, getting involved in the parish will feel more exciting and appealing.

The actual needs

Going back to an earlier point, there is a further challenge that is addressed to the pastoral council rather than to any particular ministry group. It needs to look beyond all that is currently being done, to ascertain what needs there are that are not as yet being attended to. It needs to look beyond the groups that are in existence, to begin to glimpse the groups that need to come into existence.

To do this effectively it has to engage in a very wide consultation. The people who are already involved have a certain perspective. They are often older; they are usually churchgoers; they tend to be relatively content and secure. The most effective way to identify the real needs is to ask people to name their own needs. Within such a process, people might also be more inclined to become involved in addressing their needs. And that is parish ministry.

CHAPTER 12

The Parish Pastoral Council

Questions

Two questions are imposing themselves on our parishes with great urgency today. One of them is: will our children have faith? The other is: will our parishes have priests? The first question is part of what troubles so many parents as they think of their children and of the world they are growing up in. It is made even more troubling as we see the answer to the second question inching towards a 'no'.

How are children going to have faith if our parishes do not have priests (or at least a resident priest)? We want a faith for our children that is deep and relevant, a faith that gives meaning and direction in a fast-changing world. We are beginning to realise that, in order for this to happen, we need new forms of leadership in our faith communities.

There is a third question. This question is the heart of planning for the future. It is: what is the one action which, if we did it, would make the most considerable difference to everything else about the parish? It seems to me that the answer to that question is: put in place an effective parish leadership group. I do not know of any other step that could have the same strategic impact on the future – on the question, will our children have faith?

We have been experimenting with this for decades now, ever since Vatican II first encouraged the setting up of parish councils. We have fumbled a lot, putting structures in place without any blueprint and often with only a vague sense of what we were about. But now that experience has reached a kind of critical mass. We can now gather all that experience – the cul de sacs as well as the best moments – in a way that clarifies the road ahead. Today we are within reach of enduring leadership groups that truly lead.

Why?

Some would say the reason for a pastoral council is pragmatic. The days are over when priests ran parishes on their own. The days are coming when parishes will largely run their own affairs, with the support and visits of a priest who also ministers elsewhere. If there is no pastoral council there will be nobody to take care of the parish.

But there is a deeper reason. The pastoral council is necessary pragmatically, but it is also necessary theologically. It is right. The reason we have pastoral councils today is because of the Vatican Council's insight that baptism is central. In baptism and confirmation we are all 'ordained' into a share of the responsibility for our faith community. The parish pastoral council gives expression to that truth, that we are all really responsible for all.

This fourth question, 'why a pastoral council?' is key. A clearly focused sense of role and identity is vital to successful functioning. It is also the basis for working out the structure and selection of the group. Many groups have floundered because they were never clear as to what they were about in the first place.

I will approach the role by way of gathering the experience of recent decades. Pastoral councils (or whatever else they have been known as) have taken a number of different forms. I have identified five. The learnings we can extract from these give a clear picture of what a council is meant to be like today.

Different forms

Some of the first councils took the form of finance and / or maintenance committees. It may have been a 'division of labour' mentality. People think, 'we're not trained like priests, but we can take care of the administrative end of things and free up the priest for his pastoral duties'. This, however, was not what was intended. In the 1983 code of canon law, the term 'parish council' was replaced by 'pastoral council'.

Other councils have taken the form of an advisory group. Indeed, canon law describes councils as 'consultative'. The priest gathers a group around him who will act as a sounding board, while at the same time he makes the final decisions himself. This form of council may be the best possible at a given time in a given parish, but there is more to 'consultation' than helping the priest to do his job.

In other parishes, the council has functioned as a co-ordinating committee. Members are on different sub-groups, such as liturgy, youth, communication, and the council meetings review and guide their work. A lot can get done but there is a downside. Members can identify themselves with the sub-group rather than representing the parish as a whole. Compared to the work of the sub-group, they may find council meetings de-energising. The council can become absorbed in reports from sub-groups, with a consequent neglect of longer-term issues.

Elsewhere, the pastoral council has been a reflection group or think-tank. Its energy is given to visioning, identifying needs, discerning where the gaps and possibilities are. It does not get involved in implementation, but seeks out the gifts of parishioners to form new groups to meet new needs. Not being itself directly involved in parish ministry, such a group runs the risk of losing touch and becoming a talk-shop.

Finally there are councils that have operated in a hands-on fashion. Keen to be doing something, they identify a gap and move in to fill it. For instance, they might start a parish newsletter or a family Mass. Yet, in the understandable desire to produce results, they may end up more accurately described as 'the communications group' or 'the liturgy group' rather than 'the pastoral council'.

I think that as a whole the above experience can teach us a great deal about what parish pastoral councils are meant to be and about what they are not meant to be. They suggest to me, first of all, the following five characteristics of a pastoral council.

Pastoral

The council is first and foremost a 'pastoral' group. The word 'pastoral' is about care and a listening heart. In the background is the image of the good shepherd Jesus, who had compassion for the people. If the parish can be described as a particular family of the followers of Christ, then the pastoral council is the group entrusted with the care of the parish family.

It is very important to maintain this focus. As we shall see, the 'hard' language of strategic management and planning is also part of the pastoral council. But it should not occlude the softer language of caring. The pastoral council is there to care for the well-being of the faith community. This 'pastoral' focus does not rule out an interest in buildings or administration. The well-being of the faith community has material as well as human-spiritual dimensions.

Overall

In exercising this care, the pastoral council has an overseeing role. Anybody who is on the pastoral council is there to represent and think about the parish as a whole, not any particular area of parish life. The concern of all is the overall picture and the long-term view.

If the council gets sucked into specific hands-on ministries, it is distracted from its overall perspective. If council members feel that they are representing particular groups or interests, again the overall view is lost. When you think of it, there is no other group in the parish that is asking the overall questions such as: how are things going in our parish? what does the future hold? what do we want for our parish?

Planning

The pastoral council is a planning group. It does have a role in overseeing the smooth running of the parish, but its focus is more on planning for the future. In management terms, its role is more strategic than operational. It is there to manage change. It is there to provide the leadership and vision that can help discern the way forward. It is there to identify priorities on which to focus energy and resources.

This means that the council is engaged in a different kind of 'doing' than other parish groups. For instance, there is now a huge challenge around evangelisation. There is a huge challenge around the prospect of priestless parishes. The pastoral council's 'doing' is to identify the key goals to focus on in meeting such challenges and to work out the 'roadmap' for reaching the goals. The 'doing' of others is about the practical implementation, the work of each contributing its part to the overall endeavour

Partnership

The pastoral council is not just a group that does things – caring, overseeing, planning. *How it is* is just as important as *what it does*. Earlier I spoke of the parish as a ministering community. Collaborative ministry is fundamentally about the sense of ownership and participation among all God's people. The pastoral council is a structure that gives expression to this.

This means that the pastoral council is itself meant to be an experience of the kind of church it seeks to bring about in the parish. It is permeated with a spirit of partnership, where gifts are prized, where listening is real, where decisions are shared. It is a place where collaborative ministry is experienced as synergy, an experience of God's Spirit. If it is not such a transforming experience of church for its members, it has lost its way.

Service

Finally, the pastoral council understands its leadership role in terms of service. It seeks to be true to the servant leadership that Jesus spoke of and displayed in the gospels. The council is not 'in charge' of the parish, like a kind of board of directors. The parish is in charge of the parish. The council is at the service of the parish taking charge of itself.

This spirituality of service characterises the relationship between the council and the various groups in the parish. The council is not there to lord it over groups, so as for them to say, 'Who do they think they are?' It is at their service, to affirm and encourage them in their ministry. It seeks to motivate them with a vision. It seeks to empower people and to inspire them with confidence.

The aim of the parish

If I were to synthesise all this, I would say that the role of the pastoral council is to assume responsibility for seeing that the aim of the parish is being achieved. Its activity pivots on its having an inspiring sense of the aim of the parish, a passionate sense of what the parish is called to be. It is the group with the main share of responsibility for focusing the parish on its aim and mission. It is the key group driving the process of the parish achieving its aim.

What that aim is was the focus of earlier chapters. I focused particularly on the idea of a ministering community, as being at the heart of what the parish is called to be. Ownership and participation – a vibrant sense of what it means to be baptised and confirmed, a pulsating sense of what it means to be the Body of Christ – this is at the kernel of what parish is meant to be.

The role of the pastoral council is to facilitate this, to enable this, to be at the service of this. The language here is crucial. The council is not there to achieve the aim of the parish. It is there to enable the parish to achieve its aim as a faith community. We are no longer to be a 'provided-for' church. In the past the priests provided for us. This is not to be replaced by the pastoral council providing for us. It is to be replaced by the pastoral council enabling us to provide for ourselves.

Images

One image that strikes me as apposite here is that of a *midwife*. It is the mother who has the baby, not the midwife. The midwife is there to accompany and assist and reassure. But it is not the midwife's process. Likewise in the parish: it is the faith community's own process. It is for the pastoral council to guide and encourage.

Another image is that of a *conductor*. The conductor does not play the music. It is the orchestra that performs. The conductor's role is to orchestrate, to harmonise the whole ensemble in the one movement. Similarly, the pastoral council seeks to bring scattered effort into a harmonious unity, inspired by a common vision.

Another image is that of a *moderator*. In academic life, the role of the moderator is to accompany the student writing the thesis. Some moderators impose their own ideas. But that is not the role; it is the student who writes, the moderator who supports. And in the parish, it is the faith community that is itself the agent. The pastoral council accompanies and facilitates.

A final image is that of a *navigator*. Everybody on board has their particular role in sailing the ship. The navigator's role is to ensure that we know where we are, that we know where we are going, that we plot the best route, that we have markers for determining our progress. In similar fashion, the pastoral council 'navigates' the parish, keeping an eye on the overall picture, taking care of the process in which all are engaged together.

Growing into the role
We are talking about a new and therefore unfamiliar form of leadership in the parish. It will not happen just by putting a group in place. The group has to grow into the role and that will take time, maybe a good bit of time. People will strain to get their heads around it. There will be tension between the 'doers' and the 'thinkers'. There will be frustration that success is not quick enough. There will be a temptation to become a hands-on group.

This is relevant also to leadership groups that are already in place. They too are most likely still growing into the role. Hopefully this chapter would be of use as a kind of yardstick against which to review where they are. They may recognise themselves in one of the forms of pastoral council listed. Or, in the outline of the role of the pastoral council today, they may pinpoint areas for their own growth.

The early stages

It may be helpful for the group to list the kind of things that it should be doing in its early stages. For instance, it might outline what it intends to address in its first year. Such an exercise would keep the group focused on its role and protect it from the tyranny of 'doing something'. The following are some suggestions.

Firstly, the pastoral council should put a lot of work into nurturing a spirituality of partnership. This means learning to pray together and becoming a group centred on prayer. It means learning to listen to one another and becoming open to other people's views. It means taking seriously from the start the truth that 'how we are' is critical to 'what we do'.

Secondly, it needs to spend time growing in a shared vision of parish. We cannot presume that everybody is likeminded. People come with different ideas and assumptions. There is a process of being enriched and challenged by this diversity. Growing in a shared vision, in a way that is passionate and inspiring, is the foundation for good planning. It gives depth to work that might otherwise be shallow. It could also be the basis for engaging the parish in the formulation of a vision statement.

Thirdly, the group needs to get into a good practice of communication. This has been absent so often from the work of pastoral councils. Regular quality communication with the parish will keep the agenda of renewal before people as well as contribute to building a sense of ownership. The council should contact all the groups in the parish as a gesture of interest and support. Members could function as contact persons with the different groups.

Fourthly, the pastoral council will probably need to familiarise itself with the workings of the parish. Usually the priest is the only one who has a handle on everything that is going on. Contact with the different groups will give the council a sense of what is being done. The group can move on from this to developing a picture of the needs that are facing the parish at present. To do this adequately will require some form of consultation to give voice to people's own perceptions.

Fifthly, from this visioning, communicating, familiarising and consulting, the council can begin to identify priority concerns to be addressed in the parish. They might think in terms of a strategic focus for the next three to five years. They might think in terms of an overarching theme for the coming year. That in turn will generate the work of specifying targets, resources and so on.

Sixthly, even though the council is not a hands-on group, it is important to have an early experience of achievement. Part of this is the council members' concern that people would see that they are doing something. So the above activities might include some concrete project. It could be something that the council gets done rather than does itself. But it should not be something that deflects from the main focus.

Finally, there should be review. Reasonably soon, maybe after six months, people should have a chance to say how they feel about the experience so far. This gives people a chance to check in and acts as a kind of valve to release any pent-up frustration or confusion. After a year there should be a more substantial reflection on how things are progressing. These exercises will reveal if there has been any drift from the role envisaged for the group and if there is a need to further clarify that role.

Possible questions to include in an annual review are appended. A selection from these questions could be presented as a kind of questionnaire for members to complete. Somebody would then collate the responses under each question and circulate the collated document. This would then be the basis for the group learning from its experience and charting its next steps.

PASTORAL COUNCIL ANNUAL REVIEW

Sample Questions
How do you see the role of the group?
How do you feel about your experience so far?
What has the whole experience meant to you personally?
What is your main feeling of satisfaction in the past year?
What is your main feeling of disappointment in the past year?
What do you see as the strength(s) of the group?
What weakness(es) do you see in the group?
What do you find helpful about the group's meetings?
What would you change as regards the group's meetings?
How effectively has the group grown into its role over the year?
What impact has the group had on the parish so far?
How do you feel about the quality of collaboration and decision-making in the group?
What comments do you have on the prayer element at meetings?
What comments do you have on the balance between action and reflection?
What comments do you have on the frequency of meetings?
What comments do you have on the group's membership balance (e.g. male/female, older/younger, variety of gifts and skills, aspects of parish life not represented)?
Is there any way ('in-service', training, etc) in which the group might resource itself for its work?
Other points/specific suggestions?

CHAPTER 13

Setting Up a Pastoral Council

Leadership through partnership is entering a new phase in parishes. The pastoral councils of the future are going to be true leadership groups, the core group driving the forward movement of the parish, as well as ensuring its smooth operation. The more care and thought there is put into the setting up of the council, the more likely it is that the group eventually formed will be able to deliver on the promise.

A question arises immediately with regard to the many parishes that have more than one church. Should there be one pastoral council for the parish, or separate groups for each Eucharistic community? There may be no right answer; parishes read it differently. In some cases the parish may be a rather artificial unit. On the other hand, some Eucharistic communities are very small indeed and some of the reflections that follow may need to be adapted to that context.

A task group

A very good way of going about it is to put together a task group. Its brief is threefold: to research and determine the role and structure of the pastoral council; to research and determine the selection process; to set up the initiation/orientation for the new group.

In this the task group may be starting from scratch. More likely it will not. In that case the question arises whether the previous leadership group is to be disbanded or whether it can evolve into the new role being envisaged. It may prove a delicate process. It is important, therefore, that the people on the task group are detached enough from current structures to be able to explore openly.

From the time the task group is formed to the time the new pastoral council has completed its orientation might be around six months. There is no rush and it has to be done well. It is also a formative process for the members of the task group and they might well begin their work with some time reflecting on the vision of parish that they are working towards.

A document

The task group might aim to produce a 'document'. It could be called a foundation document, or a role-and-structure document, or a reference document. But not a constitution; that sends the wrong signals about quorums and sub-committees and so on. The document might have a number of sections on: our vision for our parish; the role of the pastoral council; how the council operates; the structure; the selection process. Such a document will be invaluable to the new council in understanding itself and as a reference point in charting its progress.

In relation to the section on 'the role', I would add to the reflections of the last chapter. There should be a strong statement on the relationship between the council and the parish. The ownership of all should be to the fore, with the pastoral council seen as serving rather than providing for the parish. There might be reference to some form of regular parish assembly as a forum for developing this ownership.

This might also be some reference to the importance of a close collaboration between the pastoral council and the parish finance committee. Pastoral planning has a financial dimension and it is critical that the finance committee be in on and sympathetic to the planning mindset. Parish finances are not just about balancing the books. They are about resourcing the plans of the parish.

'How the council operates' refers to the spirituality of partnership discussed in the last chapter. It is very important that this figures prominently in the document produced, to focus the new group on the importance of prayer, of listening, of affirming gifts, of consensus decision-making.

Questions of structure

How big a group? The related question of who should be in the group is discussed later in the chapter. The trend today is towards a group of between ten and fifteen members. That size allows the group to 'gel' together well. It is small enough that everybody can feel that they are participating. It is large enough to embrace a variety of gifts and skills and perspectives. It is also large enough to function when some might be unable to attend.

A smaller parish unit may be happy with a smaller group. On the other hand, bigger parishes sometimes go for a more complex structure – besides the council, there may be a parish team running the week-to-week activities.

How frequently to meet? The question I find myself asking is: if this group is truly to be the parish leadership group, driving the whole process of planning and co-ordinating, does it not have to meet more rather than less frequently? The less often it meets, the more the real work is going to be done elsewhere (or not at all).

A monthly meeting (meaning about nine times a year) is the most common. Some groups are deciding to meet more frequently. For some, it might be worth trying fortnightly for six months and then reviewing the experience. Maybe the most significant thing here is that a good decision depends on a good discussion of what the pastoral council is about.

Next, what term of office? A three-year term is what the vast majority opt for and there is no obvious reason for making it more or less than that. The main question here is about replacing members when their term is up. The best wisdom today would point to a 'rollover' or staggered system.

The alternative to such a staggered system has been for the whole council to be replaced after three years. In that case the old council is winding down for the last six months and the new council is winding up for six months. Not only is the best part of a year lost, but there may be little or no continuity between the priorities and concerns of the old and the new council. Rollover makes for continuity.

In a rollover method, one-third of the lay members would step down each year. When the council is first set in place, it might be up to two years before the system comes into operation; otherwise some members would be stepping down after only a year. Of course, there should be no problem with the person due to step down staying on for a brief period if they are in the middle of some important project.

There are three further advantages. Firstly, it models the way things should be done. People will be more attracted to join parish groups if there is a definite and realistic time-limit. Secondly, it affords an annual opportunity for highlighting the pastoral council and its significance for the parish. Thirdly, it is an annual moment of formation for the council – any new member means that everybody is in a new group.

Selection criteria

The key factor in the selection process is getting the right group for the job. If the process fails in that the council is doomed to be an experience of frustration on all sides. The 'right group' means two things. It means, firstly, people with the appropriate gifts. It means, secondly, a good mix of people.

There are 'horses for courses'. Some people have the gifts for youth ministry, others do not. Some people are gifted for caring ministries, others are not. Some people are suited to liturgical ministry, others are not. The same is true of the pastoral council. It is not for everybody. Those on the council should be suited for the work.

I would identify the following five qualities that should characterise each and every member of the council;
- They should have the time to give; some people are already too pressured to be able to meet the time commitment.
- They should be able to think in terms of the whole parish; some people find it hard to see beyond a particular area of interest.
- They should be team people, able to work well with others, good listeners, interested on other views and perspectives; some cannot see beyond their own preoccupations.

- They should be open to new ways of doing things, with an energy and passion about the future of the parish; some hearts are mournful, some minds are stuck in the past.
- They should be able to work by way of meetings – planning, discussing, reviewing; many people who are 'doers' find meetings intolerable.

The 'right people' is also about a good mix of people. Besides the prerequisites for every member, there are other gifts that will be specific to different members of the group – the gift of youth, the gift of experience, the gift of imaginative vision, the gift of making things happen, the gift of being able to analyse and evaluate, the gift of harmonising and encouraging, the gift of translating ideas into plans, the gift of bringing the best out of others, the gift of locating resources, the gift of attending to detail.

Besides a diversity of gifts, a good mix is also about a gender balance; an age-spread; a variety of experience in ministry; people from different areas of the parish; a combination of new faces and familiar faces. If there is this mix, then there can be a real sense when the group gathers that 'the whole parish is there'. There can be a real possibility of the group 'representing' the whole parish. There can be a real confidence in the parish that this is really about all the baptised.

It will be a challenge to the parish to get 'the right people' in these different senses of the term. In particular, it will need a deliberate effort to attract younger adults, people who are not already involved, people who might feel themselves to be nearer the margins than the centre. Yet these people possess invaluable gifts for the group. They are not unwilling; it just takes determined 'marketing' to reach them.

Self-selection
The best current wisdom says that the most likely way to come up with the 'right people' is to invite people to select themselves. This is part of what I would call a 'two-moment discernment'. First, people are invited to discern for themselves if they feel called to come forward. Second, the parish discerns from those

who do come forward what would be the best combination of people for the pastoral council.

The merits of other methods are outweighed by their disadvantages. Hand-picking can produce the strongest group, but the message it sends is unacceptable. Elections, though they give a sense of ownership, carry no assurance of throwing up the right people and are almost guaranteed not to produce the right mix. Inviting parish groups to nominate members may be participative, but shares the weaknesses of elections; it also tends to end up with people seeing themselves as representing their particular patch rather than the parish as a whole.

A discernment method begins with a moment of self-selection. The key to this is getting the parish interested. The parish as a whole needs to be brought in on the process, to be engaged with it, to pray about it, to be motivated to consider it seriously, and to be provided with the information that enables individuals to discern well.

The process might be 'launched' on a particular weekend, with some 'pre-heating' over previous weekends. A presentation is made at all the Masses, preferably involving lay people, though the priest's enthusiasm should be clear. The focus is on motivating people. If, as a result of the presentation, every person in the church were to carefully consider the matter, there could be a remarkable response. 'Consider carefully' means two questions. Do I feel called to this ministry? Do I know of somebody else I think would be suitable, whom I could encourage to go forward?

This launch is accompanied by information. A brochure comes through each letterbox a day or so later, with a clear description of the role of the council, the time commitment, the gifts sought and the selection process. With the brochure comes a nomination form on which the person is asked to say what attracts them to come forward or what gifts the person they are nominating would bring to the work. There follows a period, say two weeks, when people can nominate either themselves or another (with their permission).

Parish discernment

If the presentation to the parish is enthusiastic and thorough, there will be two welcome outcomes. The quality of those coming forward will be heartening. And more people will come forward than are needed. Now comes the second discernment, this time on the part of the parish, to identify the best mix of suitable people for the work. It might be noted here that, if there is a disappointing response, a further promotion is preferable to accepting people simply because they came forward.

I think the best method here is to set up a 'search committee' – a group brought together with the job of discerning the best mix from among the nominees. They meet with all the nominees; if there is a large number coming forward, this would be divided into two meetings. The meeting has two functions. Meeting the nominees helps the search committee do its work. Discussing the role of the pastoral council gives nominees the opportunity to confirm or withdraw their nomination.

All the members of the task group might attend this meeting, plus possibly somebody from outside the parish as a statement about objectivity and transparency. This larger group can then feed into the search committee's discernment. The meeting itself might include presentations on the new council and on the selection process, a chance to mingle over a cup of tea, and discussion groups facilitated by members of the task group.

There should be a commitment to those who are not selected for the council. It should be emphasised that the process is not about choosing some people over others. All have put thought and prayer into their significant statement of commitment. Some may be future council members. Others may be involved in some specific way in the work of the council or in a particular area of parish ministry. All who have come forward have, by that very gesture, contributed to the success of the process.

Introducing the group

If parish-wide ownership of the care of the parish is to grow, the council needs straight away to insert itself close to the heart of what people see when they see 'parish'. This means making something big of introducing the council to the parish. It is not enough just to put the names in the newsletter or on the website or on the notice board and to announce it in the notices. That is all part of it, and a photograph would help too. But more can be done to express the importance of this moment in the life of the parish and to utilise the opportunity to the maximum.

One possibility is to have a parish gathering. This might best be an informal affair, maybe a chance to have a parish social. On the occasion, the members of the council can be introduced to the faith community and to all the parish groups. It is an advantage for people to meet the council before the council has done anything. It brings everybody in on it from the start. It might even be an opportunity for the council to hear some of what people want to say about their parish.

Another possibility is to have a blessing or commissioning for the new council at Sunday Mass. Alternatively, different members could be commissioned at different Masses in order to involve the whole parish. The blessing ritual is a great way of heightening awareness. It might then become an annual event, with a commissioning for new members and a renewal for those continuing their term. A sample text is included at the end of this chapter.

Orientation

Seeds need the darkness and cover of the earth in order to germinate. In like manner, the pastoral council needs some time for itself before it gets down to business. There is no rush. The parish will be repaid handsomely if the group gives substantial time to quietly setting itself up for its work. Any impulse to get 'doing' quickly needs to be firmly resisted.

What would be 'substantial' time? The group might give itself five or six sessions over a period of, say, two months. Or it might have an introductory session, followed by a full day together, followed by some further sessions. Such a commitment makes a lot of sense when one considers the goals to be achieved:

- *Group-building.* If the members enjoy being together they will work well. Gelling as a group is in some ways the main aim of the orientation sessions.
- *Role-clarity.* The group needs a level of clarity about the kind of group it is and is not, while recognising that fuller clarity will only comes with the experience of working together.
- *Vision.* This is the time to start the conversation concerning what parish is all about, what is the heart of parish, what is its mission today. Through the interaction and the diversity the group will develop an inspiring sense of purpose.
- *Agenda.* As members become clearer about the role, a sense of the group's agenda will begin to emerge. In particular, this might lead to an initial sketch of the kind of things the group would be doing in its first year.
- *Spirituality.* It is very important that the orientation include an articulation of the spirituality inspiring the group. The group needs to buy in to an ethos of partnership. The prayer element needs to be agreed. The decision-making process needs to be teased out.
- *Meetings.* Since most of the group's work will be done through meetings, some ground-rules for effective and satisfying meetings have to be established.

If the orientation sessions are built around these goals, those who come along excited but apprehensive should, by the end, have their enthusiasm and confidence strengthened for the work ahead.

COMMISSIONING RITUAL FOR A PASTORAL COUNCIL

This ritual takes place after the homily and incorporates prayers of the faithful and a creed. It is suitable either for the commissioning of a new group or for a commissioning of new members together with a renewal of existing members.

After the homily, pastoral council members are invited to come forward and form a semi-circle at the front of the sanctuary.

Introduction

Priest: We are gathered together in the presence of the risen Lord, to invoke God's Spirit on our parish pastoral council, that they may be blessed and that all of us may be enriched.

Prayers of the Faithful

Response: God of hope, bless your people

May each of us feel in our hearts the joy and peace of knowing that we are loved unreservedly by God. May all of us experience the call to use our gifts for the good of all.

May a spirit of humble service pervade the work of all who minister in our parish. May none exaggerate their importance. May none minimise their importance. May all feel appreciated for the value of what they contribute.

May this pastoral council dedicate itself to partnership in the care of our parish. May priests and parishioners grow in appreciation of each other's special vocation. May we all learn to share together the care of our parish.

May all in our parish know that they belong and experience the support of true Christian community; may all, whatever their situation, feel included and appreciated for who they are.

Action

Each parish might wish to choose for itself a symbol that reflects the significance of the work of the council – for instance, a flower, a candle, a cross, a painting ... or the parish vision statement.

Somebody from the faith community gives details of the symbol chosen. One by one, the council member come forward to the priest and take the symbol from him as he says:

Priest: Accept this [symbol],

which is a symbol of the life of our parish

which you are called to enhance and enrich.

Council member: Amen.

Blessing

Priest: We pray to God, Father, Son and Spirit,

to bless our pastoral council in its work.

May God the Father deepen your faith.

May God the Son enthuse you with hope.

May God the Holy Spirit fill your hearts with love.

All members: Amen

Creed

If the following text is not available to all, the 'Glory be' could be said instead as a short profession of faith.

Priest: I now invite all present to proclaim our faith

which gives us hope and inspires us to love:

All: We believe in the goodness of human life

and we believe in God the creator of all.

We believe in Jesus, God's own beloved;

we believe in the power of his death and resurrection

and in the triumph of good over evil.

We believe in God's Spirit, living within us and amongst us

uniting us to Jesus and calling us to love.

We believe that we all share this call

and that responding to it we can change the world.

We believe that where love is given and received

we are already experiencing our eternal delight.

Glory be ...

CHAPTER 14

Welcome to the Meeting

'The welcoming parish' probably suggests something we want to communicate to people who are nearer the margins than the centre of parish life. But it is also about those who are already involved in the parish. Strange as it may seem, people who are very involved in their parish do not always feel welcome.

I am thinking of the different groups we have been talking about in the last few chapters. I am thinking of the pastoral council and of other groups who do a lot of their work by way of meetings. To be a welcoming parish is also to be a place where going to meetings is an experience of welcome. That is not always the case.

What I am getting at here is that a group such as a pastoral council is a particular kind of group. It is not a 'committee' as we would usually understand that term. It is not just doing a job. It is a group of people who have come together as members of the body of Christ to do the work of the kingdom. The way they operate has to reflect who they are. Who they are has to be evident in *how* they are. Welcome is at the heart of this.

Caring for ourselves

A parish group that enjoys being together will do good work. If the people enjoy each other's company and look forward to being together, they experience their work as much more than a chore. But for this to be the case requires attending to how we are as a group. Many groups, in their fixation on the task in hand, have missed this entirely.

The group needs opportunities for members to get to know one another. They need an occasional cup of tea. They need an occasional social occasion, perhaps an annual dinner. They need occasional time away for prayer together. They need to take care of themselves.

If this is lacking, a feeling of warmth and welcome will also be missing. There will be the work and nothing more. But if the group does attend to itself it means that, if difficulties and disagreements arise, there will be a spirit in the group in which the problems can be addressed. There will be a sense of equality and mutual respect, making a positive outcome much more likely.

Participation

If a parish group has, say, fifteen members, the chances are that four or five of these will do most of the talking at meetings. It does not mean that the others are doing nothing. Some people engage silently but no less intensely.

But the danger is obvious. If a few are dominating the discussion the danger is that not all the gifts in the group are being brought into play. Everybody in the group should be able to say: 'It makes a difference to the group that I am here.' But if I have been here for six months without speaking or being brought in on the discussion, I may conclude: 'If I were not here, would it make any difference?'

I think of those words of John Paul II about what he called 'a spirituality of communion' – 'the ability to see what is positive in others, to welcome and prize it as a gift from God'. That is the spirit of welcome at a meeting. With that spirit all – the quiet no less than the vocal – will know and feel that their contribution is wanted. Some of those who are quiet are quiet because they do not feel that. Eventually they stop coming.

There are techniques that can help. The chairperson can interrupt a discussion and ask people to chat in pairs about the topic. If I tell you what I think and you react positively, then my confidence is boosted. I will be more inclined to share my thought with the bigger group.

Again, the chairperson can break off and go around the group for everybody's opinion. Without being put under pressure, people are being told that their view is wanted and welcome. This is particularly important if the group is making a decision. A consensus style of decision-making (as discussed in chapter six above) brings everybody in on the process and ensures that the views of a few are not mistaken for the collective wisdom.

As well as that, the whole group can be invited to become more conscious of the quality of participation. For instance, it often happens that a quieter person tries to insert something into the discussion but is swallowed up by somebody else's interjection. People in the group should notice things like that and invite each other in.

Listening

It frequently happens at meetings that people are more intent on getting their point in at the next pause than they are on hearing what is presently being said. The outcome is that points are getting piled up on top of each other, with lots of promising contributions buried and long forgotten.

Listening means that the focus is not on my view prevailing. The spirit of listening is that God's Spirit speaks through each of us and that if we do not listen to one another, neither will we hear what God is saying. If we have this disposition then we can empty ourselves when another speaks, to be available for and to welcome what they say.

But the disposition is also an art, the art of actually hearing what it is that *you* wanted me to hear. We all carry our prejudices. I presume that you mean what I think you mean. For instance, if you say 'I like going shopping', I may presume that you like spending money on new things – because that is why I like shopping. I may never get to appreciate that why you like shopping is that it gives you some relaxing time away from the hassle of the house.

If I practise being a good listener at all times, then I will bring that gift to the group meeting with me. I will be a welcoming presence. As well at that, I need to look interested. My body language has to say to you that I want to hear what you are saying, that I welcome and prize it as a gift from God.

Gifts in the group

There are different ways of 'categorising' different personalities and gifts in a group. For the purposes of this reflection, let's divide people into four types. Some people are doers, good at the practicalities. Others are harmonisers, sensitive to feelings and relationships in the group. Others are vision people, gifted with inspiring intuitions of how things might be. Others are planners, able to translate vision into steps and strategies.

Asking each member to say which of these they identify most with will tell something about the composition of the group. It will also provide an opportunity to appreciate the need for a variety of gifts. To paraphrase St Paul, 'If the whole body were doers, where would the vision be?' The group can learn, in other words, to welcome the diversity of its own giftedness. A particular concern here is for the doer and the thinker to appreciate the need for one another's gifts.

Besides this, there is a need for other balances. The gifts of youth and of experience are both needed. The gifts of both men and women are needed. The gifts brought by familiar faces and by new faces are both needed. It is important for the group to identify where it is strong and where it falls short and to go about making up what is needed.

Trust

Every group should establish a ground rule about confidentiality. For instance, a formulation that many find appealing is this: the decisions made by the group are for publication, but the discussions that lead to those decisions are private.

Such a rule gives people the freedom and the security to participate openly. They can explore, they can think out loud, they can say something that turns out to be silly, without the fear that it is going to be spread abroad or ridiculed.

It might be worthwhile for the group to talk about trust. Why is trust important? What can we do to build trust? If there is trust, people again feel welcome. There is a confidence that we all have the parish at heart. There is an appreciation, even when we argue, that we are all interested in the same thing.

The agenda

Welcome is also about having a say in shaping the agenda for the group's meeting. Sometimes the chairperson works out the agenda alone. Other times there may be a steering group planning the meeting. Obviously, good preparation means a good meeting. At the same time, the last thing anybody wants is to arrive to the meeting with the suspicion that it is being controlled by someone's personal agenda or that the discussion has been sewn up beforehand.

A simple technique is to spend the last five minutes of the meeting agreeing the main agenda item for the next meeting. Somebody can then go off to do further planning. But at least the group will now feel that it is *our* agenda. They will also know the main item in advance and have a chance to think about it. People will arrive to the meeting feeling like insiders rather than outsiders.

Review

Another way for people to feel they have a say is to make review a recurrent item on the agenda. There should be a regular 'check-in'. Maybe every few months the meeting would start by going around the group asking everybody how they are finding the experience of the group. Nothing might come up, in which case everybody may be quite happy. But that too deserves to be acknowledged.

On other occasions, though, something will come up. Checking-in functions as a kind of safety valve for releasing pent-up frustrations. Perhaps the meetings are always going over time. Perhaps the prayer is careless. Perhaps the agenda is overpacked. Perhaps people feel they are not being listened to. Checking in allows such frustrations to be expressed and addressed.

It is a way of saying to people, 'Your feelings matter enough for there to be an opportunity for you to express them.' There is more to our meeting than just the task in hand. Of course, having a check-in means that people must be willing to say what is frustrating them. If they do not say, they have to be willing to put up.

Once a year the group should engage in a more substantial review of its experience. Sample questions for such a review are appended to chapter twelve above. Again it is a way for people to have a say in how the group is evolving.

Spirituality

All of the above is about the members of the group feeling welcome in each other's company. There is one further point. It should also be evident that God is welcome at the meetings! What we are doing is more than a job. It is a collaboration with God's work in the world.

If we are working with God, then God has to be brought into the meeting too. Prayer is the main way of doing that. Quality prayer at the start or in the middle of the meeting puts the work in the context of the spirituality of the group. It invites the group into its own deepest identity.

This requires an effort. Members pray, but many will not be familiar with praying together. Some may see anything more than a cursory prayer (like the referee's whistle to start the match) as eating up valuable meeting time. But the effort needs to be made, gently yet firmly.

The chairperson

In creating this kind of ethos in the group, the role of the chairperson is crucial. Part of that person's role is about keeping the meeting focused on the task in hand and getting through the agenda efficiently. But part of it is about maximising the quality of participation and making the group a welcoming experience for all present. For this reason, many would prefer the connotations of the word 'facilitator' to those of 'chairperson'.

In choosing a chairperson, two 'don'ts' come to mind. Don't choose a chairperson straightaway. If people make the choice before they have even got to know one another, there is no telling what will happen. And don't opt for a system where each member takes the chair on a rotating basis. In all likelihood, most will make a poor job of it.

It is best to wait until the group know each other well enough and are ready to assume responsibility for themselves. They can then start the process with a discussion of what they are looking for in a chairperson. In discussing what they want in a chairperson they are also discussing what they want in a meeting. In choosing their chairperson, they are choosing to be a place of welcome where people can enjoy the task of 'growing' a welcoming parish.

CHAPTER 15

Families

Today the parish is being invited to see families as perhaps its central concern. This is not meant in an 'old-fashioned' way. From the past we are familiar with phrases like 'the family that prays together stays together', and images such as the 'holy family' of Nazareth. I am thinking more about the challenging innovative ways in which 'family' is today asserting itself at the heart of the parish agenda.

Inclusive

I put 'family' in inverted commas because how we define family is so important today. We have been used to a normative idea of family as a man and woman validly married in church, together with the children subsequently born to them. I would propose that the parish today think of family in as inclusive a way as possible.

Thinking inclusively means that all kinds of people in all kinds of situations can feel included and acknowledged. Lone parents and their children would feel included. Unmarried partners and their children would feel included. Couples in a so-called second relationship would feel included. People who are living apart from their family, childless couples, brothers and sisters living together, same sex partners, bereaved and separated people living alone – all would feel that they are acknowledged as coming from a family, belonging to a family, living family life in a particular kind of way.

Such a welcoming attitude puts the limelight on the kind of activities that are at the heart of what we call family – activities such as caring, protecting, nurturing, supporting, healing –

rather than on the structures within which those activities are practised. It allows for affirmation of the ways in which different people are realising the great human values in the diverse situations and experiences of their lives.

Already happening

It is notable how little the category of family figures in parish discourse today. When parishes identify priority areas to attend to, the same patterns repeat themselves – liturgy, outreach, hospitality, communication, youth, spirituality, adult faith, caring, evangelisation, community, and so on. Only rarely is family mentioned.

It is not that family is not present in these priorities. It is more that its presence is not taken in. It is as if the camera needs to be adjusted to bring into sharp focus a part of the picture that was vague or ill-defined. When the focus is corrected we can see that family looms very large indeed in contemporary pastoral initiatives. In fact, it is not an exaggeration to say that the most creative and life-giving pastoral innovations in today's parish revolve around families.

For a start, in many parishes, the family Mass has become the main liturgy of the weekend. Readings, music, homily, prayers are prepared with children and families in mind. There may be a special liturgy of the Word for children in a separate area. Young families feel welcome. They feel that this place is for them. Noise is welcome! People start going to Mass again. Some become involved in ministry. There is a warm atmosphere, a smile on people's faces, an air of youth and life and joy.

Likewise, the sacraments of initiation – baptism, communion and confirmation (the subject of the next chapter) – are family-focused. More and more parishes are investing serious time, planning and resources in these occasions, where families are accompanied and welcomed and prized at precious milestones in their lives. For many, the welcome they experience is the start of a new experience of church. Again, as an added bonus, people have been drawn into ministry in the process.

Again, death is a pivotal and critical time in family life to which parish ministry is paying more and more attention. Bereavement groups have been responding creatively to a huge area of need. Appreciation is growing of the value of quality work being put into the liturgies around bereavement, both at the funeral and at anniversary times. There are funeral choirs and funeral teams. Where these things are happening, there is a feeling of warmth and welcome at a time of great vulnerability.

These are some of the most familiar areas. There are also parishes that have family resource centres, where family is a very visible priority. There are parenting courses. There are the specific supports for couples preparing to get married and for couples going through difficulties in their relationship.

It all suggests that the parish of the future is one that is family-friendly. The parish of the future is family-focused. It realises that the vitality of the parish is intimately bound up with the family context in which people live their day-to-day lives.

Affirmation

It is worth elaborating on what is going on in these key areas of parish ministry to the family. First of all, what is not going on. Outreach to the family, through the family Mass, in the sacraments of initiation, at times of bereavement, is not a means to an end. It is about much more than trying to get people to go to Mass.

Rather, these outreaches are inspired by a sense that the values of the family and the values of the parish converge. The values of love and belonging, of care and solidarity, are at the heart of Christianity too. So, these outreaches are an expression of appreciation and of affirmation. They are not a means towards evangelisation. They *are* the evangelisation. If 'evangelisation' means proclaiming the good news, then here the parish is celebrating the good news about what is happening in the lives of families.

These outreaches are not about bringing people to God, or back to God. They are about the God who is *already there* in the lives of families. Very many people do not see the link. They think that God and holiness are one thing, and the ordinary affairs of daily family life quite another. They might even think that the church regards family life as an alternative option to a life of holiness, or at least as a inferior option.

These outreaches are saying that families are the primary form of the Christian life. Family life is the primary form of being involved in the faith community. It is not about getting family members involved in the parish. It is about telling them how involved they are and offering them the ministry of affirmation. In this, it is earthing words like 'vocation' and 'ministry' in the most familiar daily realities of people's lives.

This ministry of affirmation, when we think about it, cannot be left just to milestone moments in family life. It has to become the pattern of parish life. 'Parish', as we saw earlier, is about becoming a ministering community. Now we see that family is the central place where this ministering goes on. Parish life needs to revolve more and more around affirming, supporting and celebrating this.

Basic Christian community
There is a thrust today to see the parish as aspiring to become a 'community of communities'. This thrust arises from a sense that the Christian of the future is going to be somebody who has an intimate, small-group experience of being part of a community of disciples. There is an attendant apprehension that, in a post-Christian culture, it will be very hard to sustain discipleship without such an experience.

Some of the thrust comes from the experience elsewhere. In other parts of the world, where priests are in scarce supply compared to Ireland, people have had to take charge of their own faith communities. A key part of this has been organising into 'basic Christian communities', neighbourhood groups that gather to reflect on the Word of God in relation to the concerns and struggles of daily living.

Some parishes here have taken this path. But it is unlikely to become a widespread pattern in the foreseeable future. And yet the model of basic Christian communities challenges the parish in a radical way. Without such basic communities, how are people to have the kind of experience that they highlight as being crucial to discipleship?

I propose that we think of families as our 'basic Christian communities'. We will still try to attract people to participate in small group experiences focused on nurturing discipleship. But our primary concern is that each family would have a deep, joy-filled experience of themselves as a community of faith. There is no more 'basic' faith community, nor any that is as significant on our faith journey.

There are a number of advantages to this outlook. First, it includes children and young people, whereas much discourse on basic Christian communities focuses on adults. Second, it is a natural focus in that it asks for no extra commitments, no going to meetings, but rather builds on the togetherness that is already there. Third, it reflects the trend in parish life, where family is more and more seen as central to what it means to be a 'ministering community'.

The church's vision

There are good grounds in recent church teaching for taking this path of focusing on families as the basic Christian communities. In particular there are three phrases in the documents of Vatican II, which are taken up again in later papal documents.

Firstly, the family is 'a school of human enrichment'. It is the place where people learn what it means to be a human being. The experiences of attachment and security, of belonging and being loved, of being noticed and attended to, are elemental and essential to how we flourish as persons.

Secondly, the family is 'the school of the social virtues'. It is where children are gradually initiated into social relationships. It is where we learn to say 'we' and not just 'I'. Through the give-and-take of family life, we learn the basics of living in society. We learn that being a human person is about being a person-onto-others.

When we think about it, 'education' is basically about helping people to discover all that is positive and beautiful within
themselves, to realise that they are loveable and able to love, and
to open their hearts to the needs of others. As Vatican II commented, if this is not happening in the family, it is next to impossible to compensate for the loss.

Thirdly, the family is 'the church in miniature', the church in
the home. The family is itself a faith experience. Through their
human loving, they are communicating to one another the good
news of Absolute Love. Parents and children are evangelising
and being evangelised by each other. Family meals are already a
breaking of bread. Conflict resolution in the home is already a
celebration of reconciliation.

Family reveals church
There is a compelling vision in these brief texts, of the family as
both the basic human community and the basic Christian community. This means that the family is a kind of revelation or
manifestation of what 'church' is all about. Vatican II said that
the Eucharist is the primary realisation of all that the church is.
In parallel fashion the family encapsulates what faith community
is all about.

I see an important link here between the family and the
Eucharist, but one that is hardly remarked. When the priest says,
'this is my body; this is my blood', parents should recognise
themselves in Jesus' words. A multitude of mothers have silently
recognised their own experience in these words. But the loving
concern and self-giving of all parents is a daily echo of Jesus'
words.

We are used to thinking of the consecration as the living reminder of what happened on the cross. Thus we talk about the
'sacrifice' of the Mass. But it is also a reminder of what goes on at
the heart of the family. For the self-giving that goes on in the
family is a radical witness in the Christian community to what
the cross is all about.

Thus, when talking about married people, John Paul II said

that they are 'the permanent reminder to the church of what happened on the cross'. The phrase jars a little, yet it is saying something huge. When you or I, as a family member, look up at the consecration, we should see both cross and family. We should see God's love and our love, of a piece.

Again, we are habituated to making a central connection between the consecration and the priesthood. And indeed the centrality of the ordained priesthood is enduring. At the same time, as we move beyond a clerical church culture, we are learning to see family at the centre of the church. We are learning to think 'family' when we think of consecration, as an intimate aspect of its mystery.

The way ahead
The challenge today is to continue along the path that has already opened up. The family Mass, baptism, first communion, confirmation, bereavement – our experience in these areas has brought home to us again in a surprising and delightful way that family is the heart of the parish.

The way ahead is also clarified in what we have learned from these experiences. We have learned that the goal is not about getting people back to Mass, to pay more attention to 'us'. These initiatives have been fruitful because they have *not* been about expecting families to heighten their awareness of us. Rather, their fruitfulness has been about us heightening our awareness of them.

Heightening awareness of families might mean creating space for families to have a voice. Rather than doing things for families, the parish might see itself as facilitating families in doing things for themselves. The parish could then become a place where families would be enabled to respond to their own perceived needs – the needs, for instance, of young mothers, the need of care for the elderly, the need for childcare, the need for quality time.

Today's parish is called to appreciate where the Spirit is at work in people's lives. It is called to affirm that working, to give it space and encourage it – and to be evangelised by it. It is called to realise that, when it invests in families it is also investing in its own inner reality.

CHAPTER 16

Baptism, Communion, Confirmation

At present, some of the most significant and innovative ministry going on in parishes is around baptism, first communion and confirmation, as well as around the Christian initiation of adults (the latter based on the Rite for the Christian Initiation of Adults or RCIA). The adult rite reflects the original sequencing of these sacraments of initiation – baptism, then confirmation, then Eucharist – as well as the original timing, where all happened together as part of the Easter vigil.

In our experience, in contrast, initiation generally takes place in childhood, extends over a period of ten to twelve years, and has confirmation coming last in the sequence. It also constitutes something of a reversal. In the early church an adult would be converted, then instructed, then baptised and confirmed. Now we baptise the baby, we instruct the child and we hope that conversion will be the outcome!

This could well be described as the 'cutting edge' of parish ministry, the place where the challenge of evangelisation is really being taken up today. A great many of those who come forward with their children have little or no connection with the life of the faith community. Most, it seems, are reasonably well-disposed, even though on the margins. Some lack almost any sense of what it is all about.

This chapter reflects on the theological significance of the developments going on in this area. The focus is on why this area of parish life is so crucial for the future and so central to the very identity of the parish. The thrust of the reflection is towards the faith community doing its initiation in a radically new way.

An experience

I recall vividly my own first experience of the RCIA in practice.
While visiting abroad I was present at a parish Easter Vigil, during which some people (adults and teenagers) were baptised
and confirmed and others were received into the Catholic
Church.

I had never experienced anything like this before. I had been
at baptisms, but never an adult baptism. Watching another adult
take this step was like a mirror that made me unusually aware of
myself as baptised. I (and many others around me) felt a strong
sense of identity. Seeing another adult take their baptism so seriously generated a sharp sensation of 'this is who we are'.

Subsequently I found myself reflecting in the following way.
Imagine a small group of people, passionately dedicated to living out their vision, their shared beliefs and values. Imagine that
somebody from outside saw how they lived and was attracted
to find out more. Imagine this person eventually deciding to ask
if they could join the group. Imagine the response – the delight,
the honour – the desire to celebrate this event. Imagine the celebration, what it means for the newcomer and what it means to
those already in the group, as a confirmation of their way and as
a new spur to their living.

That is what every baptism is meant to be in the Christian
community. That is how central baptism is. Each newcomer is a
celebration of what we all are, revitalising our sense of who we
are, impressing on us once more the distinction of our calling. In
the RCIA this is reflected in the repeated expression of the desir-
ability of the faith community as a whole participating in the cel-
ebrations.

The same holds true with the other stages of initiation, now
separated out as first communion and confirmation. They too
are only fully what they are meant to be when they are an experience for all of us and not just for the candidates.

The reality

Let us compare this vision to the reality we experience. Think, for example, of the debate about so-called 'private baptisms'. Many couples would like to have the baptism in their own home, but this is strongly resisted. Baptism, we say, must take place in the church because it is an event of incorporation into the faith community, a communal and not a private event.

And yet, baptism as we celebrate it, is a private event! It takes place at a time when there is nobody else around in the church apart from those the family has invited. If there are a number of families, it can often feel like little more than a chaotic collection of individual, private baptisms.

'Church' in its original meaning of *ecclesia* means the gathering or assembly of baptised Christians. But there is little or no assembling here. Not alone is baptism happening apart from the assembly. In fact it is of little or no concern to anybody other than those directly involved. The 'faith community' demonstrates no interest.

Essentially it is not much different with first communion and confirmation. It looks different in that the church is full because of the numbers involved. But there is very little impact on the faith community as a whole. They may be told about it on Sunday; they may admire the children in their outfits; but again, it is of little concern to them.

All of this is, I feel, a reflection of our sense of Christian community. While there is sometimes a powerful sense of community when we gather to worship, often it feels more like a collection of individuals than a community. We have less awareness of ourselves gathering as the Body of Christ than of ourselves as individuals taking some time for our individual selves.

As long as this remains the case, the sacraments of initiation will remain private events. In this scenario, it would nearly make more sense to celebrate baptisms in people's homes and make it a quality experience of outreach and welcome. Either that or commit ourselves to a fully-fledged community model of church, as the best of current practice is inviting us to.

Three stages

I propose that we see our practice of the sacraments of initiation as being on a journey of transition that comprises three stages. The first stage is a mainly individual model of initiation. The second stage is where initiation happens in the community. In the third stage initiation is a process *of* the community.

Overall our practice is somewhere between the first and second phases. There is some great work going on in parishes to bring these sacraments into the community. But there are still many parishes where baptism is very private and communion and confirmation very much school events. Meanwhile the third stage beckons us, showing us a destination that is as yet only rarely glimpsed.

The individual model

At the core of the traditional practice that we are used to is the mindset that the sacraments of initiation are events in the life of the individual candidate. Further, they are actions that are done to the individual. In baptism, according to this mindset, the individual is cleansed of original sin. Next, the individual boy or girl receives holy communion. Finally, he or she has the gifts of the Holy Spirit bestowed on them.

In the past, baptism was so private and individual that we went ahead even if the mother was still confined and unable to be there! The thing was to get the child cleansed, and as quickly as possible. In the case of communion and confirmation, the tradition has been that the school took care of things. The role of the parents and of the parish was minimal.

In the community

In the second stage, initiation is seen as taking place in the community. This introduces a theme of collaboration. The celebration of baptism is based on a co-operation between the family and the parish. The celebration of first communion and confirmation represents a partnership between school, home and parish. These transitions mark a notable shift in how we understand what is going on.

Baptism is now understood in terms of incorporation into the Christian community. While Christ's victory over sin is central to this, the emphasis now is on welcome and belonging. I recall the surprise and pleasure of one mother as she exclaimed; 'I never realised that baptism had anything to do with welcome!' She had presumed it was just a job to be done.

The shift to welcome is reflected in the emergence of parish baptism teams. Members of the team visit the families, to convey welcome and to go through the ceremony. There may be meetings for groups of parents, sometimes run by other young parents, again with the stress on welcome. Members of the team then accompany the family at the ceremony, so that they feel at home. The number of baptisms at the same ceremony may be restricted in order to enhance the homeliness.

Throughout, there is a strong sense of the home as the basic Christian community. But there is also an aspiration to link baptism in more closely with the larger faith community. The newly baptised are prayed for at Mass; they are welcomed in the newsletter; their photos are displayed in the church. Occasionally during the year baptism may take place at the Eucharistic assembly, for instance at the Easter Vigil or on the feast of Our Lord's Baptism.

With communion and confirmation, the trend now is towards their preparation and celebration being headed up by the parish. Partnership between parish, home and school is key, but increasingly the main responsibility is seen to lie with the parish and the home. The school's role is to resource this process in a very special way. But it is not the school's process.

With both sacraments, the trend is towards an elaborate year-long programme, with a substantial investment of time, energy and personnel. A lay pastoral worker may be engaged. Parent leaders are trained. There is an enrolment ceremony in the church, followed by a programme of 'Faith Friends', parent meetings and home visits, paraliturgies and retreats. In some cases, the sacramental event itself is incorporated into the Sunday Eucharist.

As with baptism, the stress all through is on welcome and affirmation. For example, one parish produces a video of the children in school to show to the parents. It is done as a way of affirming that the values driving the sacramental programme are the same values as those cherished by the parents themselves.

We can see in all these initiatives a growing conviction that the sacraments of initiation are to be situated in the life of the whole faith community. We can see concrete ways in which this is beginning to find expression. But it is just beginning. While initiation is beginning to happen in the community, there is a journey to be travelled before it is owned by the community.

Of the community

In the third stage this ownership is being acknowledged. Initiation is seen as a process within the community. Just as these moments are milestones in the journey of the family, so are they highpoints for the community as a whole. Not alone do they take place in the community, they are embraced as experiences of the community.

This is absolutely critical. Initiation is not simply something that happens in an individual's life. It is something that happens to a community of faith. On the one hand, the individual is engaged on a journey of initiation into the community. On the other, the community is engaged on a journey into initiation itself. Only when the latter is happening is initiation what it is meant to be. This is the idea in the RCIA, when it says that the Lenten catechesis is meant to renew the whole faith community.

Initiation never ends. As a faith community we are ever exploring, ever penetrating more deeply into the mystery of who we are in Christ Jesus. Whenever another individual begins the process of initiation or progresses to the next milestone, the whole community sees itself mirrored and hears its own calling echoed. Each time it is a grace and a sacrament for all, when all are born anew and inspired anew and joined anew as the Body of Christ. Each time it is a commitment to care for the newly initiated.

Elements of this are already present, whenever a baptism is celebrated as part of Sunday Eucharist, or when first communion takes place on Sunday, or when RCIA is going on in the parish. But it is only happening when these events are the occasion of a mindset shift on the side of the community, towards a radical ownership of its own baptismal reality.

Size is a handicap in all this. It is easy to imagine when the group is small and alive to its own identity, when there is occasionally a newcomer and where this is greeted enthusiastically. You can see then how big it could be and how incomprehensible it would be for the initiation to happen apart from the group in any way.

The challenge lies in translating that model into the context of larger communities, where neophytes are more frequent and where there is a weaker sense of identity and solidarity. But we can see from the above how it is already happening, how some parishes are forging ahead, with enough experience gained for others to confidently join in. The key, though, may be to realise that baptism, communion and confirmation are less about evangelising the candidate's family than about the community being itself evangelised into its true identity.

A policy question

The theology and vision articulated here needs also to be reflected in actual church policy regarding those who present for the sacraments of initiation. As we know, those who bring their children for these sacraments include many whose participation in or allegiance to Christian faith community is either tenuous or token. It is unsatisfactory that each parish acts alone in their regard. What follows are some suggestions that might form the basis of a united approach.

First of all, there are two values at stake. On the one hand, there is the integrity of initiation itself. Theologically it is hugely significant for the faith community and demands to be treated with the utmost seriousness. Any devaluing of it should be felt to be a scandal. On the other hand, there is the pivotal place of welcome within all pastoral ministry today. The judgemental attitudes of the past have given way to our embracing God's own value of inclusiveness.

Extreme views ignore one or other of these values. Some would simply accept all-comers freely; their very coming forward would be taken as signifying intent. This view undervalues the integrity of initiation and glosses over the fact that some who come forward are not well disposed. Others, in contrast, would set in place firm conditions around preparation courses and such like. This view lacks appreciation of where people may be at and can contribute to an exclusive and alienating atmosphere.

A satisfactory approach seeks to combine both values. In this approach, welcome is the first word that people hear, because that is what the church is meant to be, a reflection of God's own welcoming heart. Any contact with church is meant to be an inviting experience of affirmation. In the spirit of the prodigal son story, the parish opens its arms to any who come in its direction.

In many cases people already feel a sense of belonging. In many other cases, the hope is that the positive experience of welcome and affirmation will touch people's hearts with something of the truth of the gospel. Whether it does or does not cannot be controlled. It is a matter of doing what we believe is right and trusting in a good action to bear its own fruits. And what we believe is that the church is called to be God's welcoming heart in the world.

But there are cases where something further is appropriate. Where Christian initiation clearly has no meaning for the parents, where it may even go against their explicit beliefs, a process of discernment is called for. Otherwise both they and the parish are in conflict with their conscience.

Ideally there would be no need to resort to a refusal. Preferably in such cases people would themselves freely withdraw in the light of the discernment. Then the conversation would have yielded a 'win-win' situation, each party satisfied that they were being true to themselves.

With first communion and confirmation, though, there is a further ingredient, namely that the child is old enough to express their own preference. That preference may be influenced by peer pressure, but may well reflect also the way in which the catechetical programme has touched their heart. Here we do well to remember the words of Paul VI, that evangelisation works both ways. It is not just that parents communicate the gospel to their children but they also receive the gospel from their children, who may be living that gospel in quite a deep way. These are times in which that form of evangelisation is becoming more significant.

CHAPTER 17

Adult Faith

Most would agree that adult faith and its development should feature prominently in parish planning today. There is particular concern about what is happening to faith in younger adults and up to middle-age. Despite this concern, there can be a lack of clarity about what is involved and how to respond. Perhaps the first step we can take is to develop our way of thinking about adult faith and how it grows. That in turn can act as a basis for practical planning.

More than talks
The way we talk about adult faith can be more of a hindrance than a help. We tend to associate adult faith development with talks and courses, whether in the parish or at some central venue. For instance, the parish might organise a series of weekly talks for Lent or a short course introducing some aspect of theology or scripture. We seem to think about it as something for the head, an intellectual affair.

Twenty or thirty or forty people might participate and go away satisfied. The evidence seems to suggest that if something similar is offered the next year, more or less the same twenty or thirty or forty people will reappear. In other words, while such initiatives are valuable and worthwhile, their appeal seems to be quite limited. More is needed in order to address the concerns we feel about adult faith.

The language we use does not help. We speak of 'adult education'. The word 'education' suggests something quite formal. It may also be alienating for those whose experience of formal education was negative. We also speak of 'adult faith formation'.

While 'formation' embraces more than the intellectual, it is doubtful if most people would know what we mean by the term.

Integration

'Adult faith' is more than the intellectual understanding that a focus on talks and courses suggests. That focus may itself be related to a traditional Catholic conception of faith, which cast it in terms of intellectual adherence to revealed truths. In that conception, a growth in knowledge was the dimension highlighted in the growth of faith.

Today a good way of speaking about adult faith or mature faith is to see it as an integration of faith and living. Paul VI said that 'the split between the gospel and culture is without a doubt the drama of our time'. Gospel and culture; faith and life; the holy and the ordinary – in recent times these have become strangers to one another. The split affects each one of us. The challenge to the parish is to help re-introduce them again as familiar friends.

I recall being involved in conducting a survey in a parish about adult faith. People were asked (at Mass) to tick which of a list of twelve areas they saw as their own greatest need. The areas listed were: how to pray; scripture and theology study; finding God in suffering; role of laity in the parish; exploring my own spiritual journey; adult understanding of faith; preparing for ministry; prayer in the family; where is the church going?; linking faith and justice; women in the church; nourishment for couples / parents.

Out of about 750 responses, well over half put one of the items to do with prayer and the spiritual journey as their first preference. Scripture and theology were down the list. Involvement in ministry was at the bottom.

It was a striking statement. The basic needs of adult faith are personal and experiential. People want help with their spiritual search. They want to be able to reflect on their life experience in the light of faith. They want faith to throw light on their daily living. When that need is being satisfied, questions of theology and ministry may become interesting. But the key is that personal connecting, that spiritual search.

Qualities of adult faith

Adult faith is happening when this integration is happening, when faith and ordinary living are friends rather than strangers, mirroring each other rather than opaque to one another. The connecting of faith with life can be broken down into a number of important aspects. These might be seen as some of the key qualities of an adult faith.

The first of these qualities is ownership. When faith and life connect, people take ownership of their own faith and their own faith journey. This means that they can take ownership of and responsibility for their own baptism and confirmation, sacraments which so often appear to be no more than dim and distant memories.

Ownership reflects what has been called the shift from 'the experience of authority' to 'the authority of experience'. The culture of being told what to think and do has yielded to a culture where we learn to explore our own experience and trust in our own inner wisdom. But it can be a painful journey; some do not wish to begin; others do not know it is possible.

Prayer and reflection is a second quality, following from this. Adult faith is characterised by a quality of prayer, deliberation and reflection in one's life. The experiences of daily life are seen and interpreted in terms of one's faith. In turn, one's daily living becomes more and more reflective of one's faith. The Word of God comes to centre stage, as an internal dialogue develops between scripture and personal experience. There is a growing intimacy with Jesus Christ that is grounded in the ups and downs of ordinary everyday life.

A third quality has to do with community. An owned, reflective adult faith, while highly personal, is not private. Adult faith is shared faith. It means participation in the community of disciples. This includes a feeling of belonging to and identifying with the faith community. It includes a sense of shared responsibility for the well-being of the community. It includes participation in the communal worship. It may include engagement in some specific ministry within the community.

Love and justice are words for a fourth quality. Part of the living sense of being a member of the Body of Christ is a lived conviction that a Christian life has its centre of gravity outside the self. The person of adult faith hears the 'call' of the other and lives their life in an ever more sensitive responsiveness to others. This sensitivity expands into a passion about questions of justice in society. They find their life caught up in Jesus' own passion for God's kingdom.

The practising Catholic

This is just one person's sketch of the qualities of adult faith. It leads me to reflect again on that phrase, the 'practising Catholic'. I said above that talk of adult faith sometimes narrows it down to its intellectual element. In this phrase too there is a narrowing down. Our usage of the term 'practising Catholic' sees faith only in terms of its worship component.

But if we think of 'adult faith' instead of 'practising Catholic', the picture broadens out to include the above themes of ownership and responsibility, prayer and reflection, belonging and participation, love and justice. This in turn suggests that there are many more people 'practising' than we suppose!

Some people's faith involves little more than going to Mass. Other people's faith is full of service but is lacking in prayer and communal worship. All of us will find ourselves challenged in some way by the richer notion of a practising Catholic. It may be a surprise to think that the person who goes to Mass and the person who does not are both practising – and both in need of practising in a fuller way.

A further important aspect of this is that adult faith is a lifelong journey. There is no end point other than death itself. There is no point at which faith has reached maturity. The conversation between faith and living continues, growing ever deeper. We are all lifelong learners, for ever being initiated further into the mysteries of human and Christian living. When we think we have arrived is when we are furthest from our destination.

Where to start?

A good place to start addressing the needs of adult faith in the parish would be to do an inventory of what is already happening. If we think 'adult education' there may be quite little going on. But if we think 'adult faith', we will find that there is already quite a deal of faith enrichment going on. Consider the following and see if it clarifies our way forward.

Adult faith is being enriched whenever liturgy meets life. Whenever liturgy helps a person make the connection between their life experience and what they believe, there is a growth in faith. It may happen on a special occasion such as a family funeral or an anniversary Mass, a first communion or a parish novena. At such moments the thirst of the spirit is nourished and the milestones of life are dignified.

Sunday Eucharist is the greatest source of such enrichment. It really is the single most important occasion for sustaining and enriching faith, for affirming the God that is in everyday, for deepening the sense of discipleship. Overall, though, we are not unlocking this potential. Those with a solid, secure faith can find enrichment in a routine celebration of Eucharist; they have the inner resources. But many more require help; it has to be made relevant and enriching for them.

Adult faith is being enriched whenever people experience welcome and belonging. This happens when resources are invested in preparing baptism, first communion and confirmation with care and imagination. It happens when there is a creative family Mass. It happens with all those caring outreaches that say to people, 'we notice that you are there and we care that you exist'.

Adult faith is being enriched through the experience of being involved in ministry. Faith is in our hands as well as in our hearts and heads. When we do something, or when we are asked to do something, we discover our giftedness. We find our faith is enhanced and our conviction strengthened when we experience ourselves as giving and as helping build Christian community.

Adult faith is being enriched when a person has the experience of belonging to a small group, a prayer group for instance, or a group focused on service. This group, which may not be parish-based, may be a very significant element in the person's living out of their faith and in their deepening sense of discipleship.

And, of course, adult faith is enriched through talks and courses. Enrichment is more likely when such provisions are clearly related to people's own felt needs – for instance, their needs around bringing up children, or coping with suffering, or wanting new ways to pray, or being involved in a parish ministry group.

My own conviction from all this is that the heart of adult faith development is about a positive, welcoming experience of Christian community where people are enabled to make the links between faith and life. This means that adult faith development is primarily a process of 'socialisation' into faith community. When this is happening, people are already coming to a new understanding and appreciation of what it means to be a Christian. Talks and courses can build on this; rarely if ever can they supply for it.

A priority

The challenge is to make adult faith enrichment an explicit and deliberate parish priority. The Rite for the Christian Initiation of Adults points the way. It brings to us today a sense of the central position that adult faith initiation occupied in the early Christian community. We begin to realise how this was gradually lost until, in recent centuries, the focus had shifted almost entirely to the faith development of children.

Church documents today are re-affirming the priority of adult faith development. Two reasons are presented. On the one hand, without taking away from the integrity of childhood faith, only adults are capable of a fully developed faith. On the other hand, adults have the greatest responsibilities in communicating faith to others.

This emphasis reflects the shift that has been taking place since Vatican II, from a church characterised by paternalism to one characterised by participation. An egalitarian church, stressing the baptism call of all, demands a new kind of adult faith along the lines I have been outlining. The new style of church cannot happen without a new kind of adult faith – or rather, without a new, *adult kind* of faith. An adult kind of adult faith is an indispensable foundation of tomorrow's church.

While Vatican II has seen an eruption of movement in this area, there is a long way to go. Huge numbers have participated in various courses and processes. Many have become qualified in theology, catechetics, scripture, spirituality. At the same time, for many, many others there remains a dichotomy. In secular life they may have progressed to an academic or professional qualification. But their religious development may not have progressed beyond primary school level.

Obstacles

There are a number of obstacles in the way of baptised adults progressing to an adult kind of faith. Some of them have to do with the church. Some of them are more internal to individuals.

The culture of paternalism has not disappeared. People are not everywhere treated as equals nor invited to take responsibility for their own faith and their own church. Even where they are, the power of prior conditioning means that not everybody is willing to accept the invitation.

One reason for this is the fear that any openness to a more adult faith will threaten childhood certainties. Some people are afraid to move from comfort to exploration. Thus we have a strange situation. On the one hand, it is not always clear that the church wants people to have an adult kind of faith. On the other, not everybody wants it for themselves.

Another obstacle is the impression that religion is for children. All the resources put into school catechesis can create this impression, that religion is something you move on from when you become an adult. The impression is reinforced wherever a paternalist style of church continues to treat adults as less than adults.

Another obstacle is language. Church discourse (in the liturgy for example) is often carried on in a language that is quite distant from everyday life. The God of that language can seem very far way away, a God and a language that only theologians could understand. So, for many, language alienates from church and ultimately from their own spirituality. It prevents rather than facilitates making the links that would integrate faith and living.

All these obstacles have one thing in common. It is about baptised adults being treated as adult Christians. For baptised adults to treat themselves as adult Christians means a determination to transcend a childhood faith and to embrace the adult kind of faith that is possible today. But this in turn challenges church and parish to treat baptised adults as adult Christians, respecting their experience, talking their language and stimulating their co-responsibility.

Becoming articulate

Before concluding I want to return to the intellectual theme. Faith today is seen primarily in terms of the heart – as a relationship to Jesus – and of the hands – as a call to action. But there is also a 'head' element, to do with understanding. It has a particular relevance today.

There was a 'doctor knows best' quality to the paternalism of the past. Priests understood the theology; lay people just did and thought as they were told. But today, when the culture is no longer uniformly Christian, that leaves people at a loss. In a pluralist milieu, when there are other identities, other self-understandings around, faithful Christians struggle to articulate who they are and what they believe.

So a crucial dimension to adult faith development is to build on the foundations of a sense of ownership and belonging, so as to enable Christians, in the words of St Peter, to be able to give an account of the hope that is in them (1 Peter 3:15). But it is mainly by talking and sharing with one another that we will become articulate.

Two images

In conclusion, two images for adult faith, from Mark's gospel. The first image has to do with sight. It suggests that the faith journey is a lifelong process of enlightenment. Significantly, the early church spoke of those to be baptised as 'those to be enlightened'. We are a learning community, constantly being initiated. The experience of community is itself enlightening and formative of faith.

> Some people brought a blind man to him and begged him to touch him. He took the blind man by the hand and led him out of the village; and when he had put saliva on his eyes and laid his hands on him, he asked him, 'Can you see anything?' And the man looked up and said, 'I can see people, but they look like trees, walking.' Then Jesus laid his hands on his eyes again; and he looked intently and his sight was restored and he saw everything clearly. (Mark 8:22-25)

The second image has to do with hearing and speaking. Significantly again, the passage is part of the baptism ritual. It suggests that baptised Christians are always learning to hear and to speak, always being released from deafness and incoherence, to become articulate and eloquent in bearing hope to the world.

> They brought to him a deaf man who had an impediment in his speech; and they begged him to lay his hand on him. He took him aside in private, away from the crowd and put his fingers into his ears and he spat and touched his tongue. Then looking up to heaven, he sighed and said to him, 'Ephphatha,' that is, 'Be opened.' And immediately his ears were opened, his tongue was released and he spoke plainly. (Mark 7:32-35)

The last thing we should presume is that adult faith development is something that 'they' need. We begin by realising that we are all blind, deaf, incoherent. Maybe the first thing in understanding the issue of adult faith is to be in touch with our own faith needs as adults.

CHAPTER 18

The Ministry of the Word

Those who proclaim the scripture at Mass could be forgiven for feeling a little like second class citizens, when placed alongside ministers of the Eucharist. The latter have a grander title compared to mere 'readers'. They also have a commissioning ceremony, unlike readers.

However, this simply reflects how peripheral the Word has been compared to the Eucharist. Recall how, in the past, one only needed to be present from the time of the Creed to have fulfilled one's Sunday obligation. The Mass was the Eucharist, the consecration.

Indeed, in the past, the Bible was a book that Protestants read. One priest tells a story from around 1960 of how a parishioner called to his door asking permission to buy a Bible! The incident suggests how it might actually have been dangerous to have or read a Bible. Until a few decades ago, even priests knew very little about it.

All this is by way of coming to the point that the ministry of the Word in the parish deserves far greater reflection and attention. Proclaiming the Word at Mass is one part of that ministry, but only a part. It points to the ministry of the Word that lies at the heart of our lives as individuals and as members of the faith community.

A change of mindset

The Vatican Council marked a change from the second-class status of the Word. Consider the following passage as an indication of how radical a change was taking place:

'The Church has always venerated the holy scriptures, just as she venerated the Body of the Lord. She never ceases, especially in the Eucharist, to partake of the bread of life and offer it to the faithful from the one table of the Word of God and the Body of Christ.'

This is a huge shift. It is asking us to think of the Word of God at Mass as a 'real presence', just as we think of the Body of Christ. The 'bread of life' is both the Body of Christ and the Word of God. The Word feeds and nourishes. The Word is life. The Word is made flesh. Today we talk of 'the table of the Word', in order to indicate the status of the Liturgy of the Word alongside the Liturgy of the Eucharist.

It is also part of a broader shift. For instance, in talking about the ministry of the priest, Vatican II says that the 'first task' of priests is to preach the gospel of God to all people. We had been used to thinking that the 'apex' of priestly action was the consecration. And while it is not a matter of 'either-or', this is certainly asking us to think again. It is asking us to think of the ministry of the Word (or 'evangelisation') as the heart of what the church is about.

We have still quite a journey to travel. Scripture remains a distant thing for most Catholics. Mass is still the consecration. The Word is a long-winded, often unintelligible prologue. The Bible does not figure in people's lives or prayer. This cannot but be a big handicap in the challenge of integrating faith with daily living, a theme highlighted in the previous chapter.

Word made flesh
We need to form some basic perspectives on this situation. First of all, Christianity is a religion of the Word. Its good news for the world is that 'the Word became flesh' (John 1:14). It is called on to proclaim this good news. Without the word of proclamation, the Word made flesh will not be heard. Nobody comes to know Jesus without the mediation – the 'word' – of other people (see Romans 10:14-15).

The Word is what creates Christian faith community. As Vatican II puts it, the people of God is formed into one in the first place by the Word of the living God. The faith community could be defined as a group of people who have heard the same Word and who together share its joy and take up its challenge. The Word becomes flesh whenever faith community is formed.

While the appreciation of scripture in the parish is generally weak, that is not to say that the Word is not alive and active. The Word is being made flesh in all kinds of ways every day. Wherever and whenever a person's faith inspires them to care and solidarity, the Word is made flesh. Wherever and whenever the faith community communicates welcome and belonging, the Word is made flesh. It is just that people do not appreciate this as they might.

The fifth gospel

I think it was St Francis de Sales who said that there is no more difference between the written gospels and the lives of saints than between written music and music sung. Each Christian is like a 'fifth gospel'. Each Christian life is an original proclamation of the Word, the good news. St Augustine echoes the same sentiment:

> 'The one who has learned to love a new life has learned to sing a new song. A new person, a new song and a new testament all belong to the same kingdom. My children, holy seeds of heaven, you who have been born again in Christ, born from above, 'sing to the Lord a new song'. Sing with your voices, sing with your hearts, sing with your lips, sing with your lives. Be yourselves what you speak. If you live good lives, you are God's praise.'

This astounding truth indicates that our spirituality should be rooted in scripture. It echoes the occasion when Moses tells the people to keep the words he has spoken in their hearts. They are to recite them to their children and to talk about them at all times, wherever they are. They are to 'bind them as a sign on your hand, fix them as an emblem on your forehead and write them on the doorposts of your house and on your gates' (Deuteronomy 6:6-9).

Christians are meant to be people who are married to the Word, who immerse themselves in it, who listen intently to it, who live from it, who pray with it, who measure themselves by it. In this way they become a fifth gospel. Their lives incarnate what the four written gospels say. Other people hear in their lives the song that is the good news.

Ministry of the Word in the parish
The ministry of the Word in the parish is first and foremost a ministry to be exercised by each baptised person. It is the ministry of being a 'fifth gospel'. Secondly, in a more specific sense, the ministry of the Word is about specific actions in the parish that enable people to become the fifth gospel.

The main such action is the Liturgy of the Word within the Eucharist, which includes the 'readings' and the homily. As things stand, there is much to be done in order that the passages from scripture be a welcoming experience for the assembly. More often than not they are an alienating experience, which is an incredible state of affairs for a religion based on the Word. When scripture is not proclaimed slowly and clearly it is rendered even less welcoming.

The homily is one element in making scripture an inviting experience. It is not the only element, but it is an extremely important one. This is the point in the Mass where a bridge is built between the Word and people's lived experience. The priest may not be a born orator, but if he is deeply connected both with the Word and with people's lives he will have a lot to say. But given that it is such a pivotal ministry, it makes no sense that the gifts and perspectives of lay people are not brought more into play.

Looking outside the liturgy, scripture-based shared prayer and reflection is a form of the ministry of the Word with great potential for forming people in the Word. *Lectio divina* ('divine reading') is one such, where people take a passage from the Bible and work through a number of steps in order to enter into its meaning, hear its message and relate it to their lives.

There are other ministries of the Word which are of a more educational kind. Parish-based scripture study groups and courses in academic centres have great potential for enrichment, even if few tend to be attracted. For young people, those responsible for religious education in schools are ministers of the Word also, even if the effectiveness of their ministry grows more problematic by the year.

Again it is clear that we have quite a journey to travel. Access to scripture, says Vatican II, ought to be wide open to all Christians. Scripture should be leading all into the joy of knowing Christ. But as it stands, the words of St Jerome continue to confront us: 'Ignorance of the scriptures is ignorance of Christ.'

Ministers of the Word

There is a move away from talking of 'readers' to talking of 'ministers of the Word'. The phrase may be more unwieldy, but the change is welcome. It signals the dignity and importance of this function. It highlights the status of the Liturgy of the Word. It affirms that the Word is at the heart of what we are.

In the same spirit, we talk of these ministers 'proclaiming' rather than 'reading' the Word. We read the notices but we proclaim the scriptures. 'Proclaim' indicates that something is happening. As Isaiah puts it, God's Word does not return to God empty; it accomplishes that for which God intended it (Isaiah 55:11). When the minister proclaims, God's Spirit accompanies and acts. When you proclaim, God acts in me. God is working in you, for me.

This takes us to the heart of what this ministry is all about. I said in an earlier chapter that all particular ministries have as their essential purpose the building up of a ministering community. Ministry is not just doing something 'for' others. It is enabling others; it is activating their ministry. Likewise, ministers of the Word function for the sake of a ministering community. Their purpose is not to provide information, as do the notices. It is not to have another voice alongside the priest's. Their purpose is to serve, to enable.

What they are enabling is 'the fifth gospel'. The minister proclaims the Word in order to assist you and me to make the connections between the Word of life and our own experience of life. So there are two levels to what is going on. On a surface level there is the audible proclamation. Beneath the surface this proclamation is the occasion of the Word taking root and growing in people's hearts. It is enabling the hearer to become a fifth gospel, to sing the new song with their lives.

Keeping the ministry alive
But there is a real danger that this ministry becomes just a routine, 'reading' and nothing more. It is different from other ministries like a baptism or bereavement team, where there is a vitalising personal contact. It is more like ministers of the Eucharist, prone to being thought of as just a job to do or a function to perform. This presents a challenge to both the minister and the parish, to keep the meaning of the ministry alive.

Two things are required of the ministers themselves. The first is for their lives to be in living relationship with the Word. This includes serious preparation with the passage they are to proclaim – spending time with it, possibly consulting a commentary, praying for awareness of its power, reading it aloud.

More deeply it involves an ever more intimate relationship with scripture, in the spirit of the words of Moses quoted above. This could, for instance, take the form of a daily conversation, taking a passage such as the gospel of the day to pray with and relate to one's own life. In some such way, scripture must be moving more and more towards the centre of the minister's self-understanding.

The second requirement is for ministers' lives to be in living relationship with the faith community for whom they proclaim the Word. I am thinking here of the passage where Jesus saw the people and 'had compassion for them because they were like sheep without a shepherd and he began to teach them many things' (Mark 6:34). Before he speaks, Jesus feels compassion. He speaks out of his compassion.

In the same spirit, ministers of the Word might think of and pray for those to whom they proclaim. They might try to connect compassionately with where people are at. The text to be proclaimed could help. The minister can reflect on where its themes surface in people's lives – themes such as sorrow and struggle, peace and tranquillity, anger, loneliness, fear, hope, love, lostness, thirst, desperation, determination. This will help in appreciating the text. The compassion engendered will communicate itself in the proclamation.

A diagram may help. The above two relationships are represented by two sides of the triangle. First there is a living relationship between the minister and the Word. Second there is a living relationship between the minister and the people. If these two 'lines' are active, then the third side of the triangle will be helped 'happen', through the power of the Spirit. People will connect with the Word. It will link with their lives and take root in their hearts. They will be enabled to become 'the fifth gospel'.

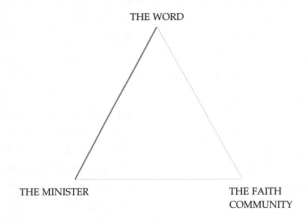

The parish
It is not all up to the ministers. The parish has an important role in caring for ministers of the Word and supporting their ministry. This begins by ensuring that all begin their ministry with good preparation, addressing both the spiritual aspect and the practicalities of effective proclamation. As a way of highlighting

the status of the Word, the ministry might begin with a blessing before the assembly; a sample text is appended.

An emphasis on quality might include advocating to each minister that he or she find themselves a mentor. This means approaching somebody they trust, who would be willing to give them feedback on an ongoing basis. There will be little or no feedback otherwise. Such an arrangement would also help the individual to recognise if, for instance, their voice has become too weak through age.

Initial preparation is often all that ministers of the Word get. They also need to be resourced and accompanied. The parish might try to ensure that each one has a copy of the Bible, or a missal, together with access to useful commentaries. There might be occasional sessions for ministers, for their own enrichment and for practical updating. There might be an annual re-dedication, using a ritual such as that below.

Finally, in the preparation of individual liturgies, there is much that the parish can do to enhance the unity of the Liturgy of the Word as a whole. The introduction to the Mass, the readings, the homily, the prayers, all belong together. If they are planned as a unit, so that people experience them as a unit, the power of the Word will be released.

The ministers of the Word are a very important and valuable presence in the faith community. They are a sign to all that we are formed as a community through the power of the Word. Their presence is a statement – as yet far too softly spoken – that we are called each to be a 'fifth gospel', so that the Word may become flesh and live among us.

A BLESSING RITUAL FOR MINISTERS OF THE WORD

After the homily the priest invites those ministers present to approach the sanctuary and stand in a semi-circle

Introduction
We are gathered today in the power of God's Holy Spirit
to honour the Word of God,
the Word proclaimed for us to hear,
in which God is truly present
and whereby God comes to us and makes a home with us.

Prayers of the Faithful
We pray for our ministers of the Word
who serve us by proclaiming the Word to us;
May they be enthusiastic in their ministry. Lord hear us.

We pray for all of us who hear the Word;
May it find a home in our hearts;
May it connect with our lives;
May it nourish and encourage us;
May it give us meaning and direction. Lord hear us.

The Word of God is filled with the power of the Spirit
and proclaims Good News for the world;
We pray that this Spirit will bring joy to people who are sad
and hope to people who are desolate
and courage to people who are afraid. Lord hear us.

Lectionary
Each minister approaches the priest individually and takes the lectionary in their hands.
Priest: Receive the book whose Word you are to proclaim;
Treasure it in your heart; honour it in your life.
Minister: Amen. *(returns lectionary to priest)*

Blessing of all ministers
May God the Father bless you in your ministry.
May God the Son speak his Good News through you.
May God the Holy Spirit live in all who hear you.
All: Amen

Profession of Faith
Priest: Let us all proclaim together our faith
which give us hope and inspires us to love;
All: Glory be to the Father and to the Son and to the Holy Spirit
as it was in the beginning, is now and ever shall be, world without end. Amen.

Ministers return to their seats.

BEANNÚ MINISTÉIRÍ AN BHRIATHAIR

Taréis an tsearmóin, tugann an sagart cuireadh do na ministéirí atá i láthair teacht chuig an tsanctóir agus seasamh i leath-chiorcail.

Réamhrá
Táimíd cruinnithe inniú i gcumhacht Naomh Spiorad Dé
chun onóir a thabhairt do Bhriathar Dé,
an Briathar atá fógartha dúinn a chloisteáil,
ina bhfuil Dia i láthair go fírinneach
agus ina dtagann Dia chugainn
agus ina ndéanann Dia dídean linn.

Guí an Phobail
Guímís ar son ministéirí an Bhriathair a fhreastlaíonn orainn
tríd an Bhriathar a fhógairt dúinn.
Go raibh siad díograiseach ina ministreacht. A Thiarna éist linn.

Guímís ar son gach duine againn a chloiseann an Bhriathar;
go bhfaighe sé dídean inár gcroíthe; go nasca sé lenár saol;
go gcothaí sé is go spreaga sé sinn;
go dtuga sé miniú and treoir dúinn. A Thiarna éist linn.

Tá Briathar Dé lán le cumhacht an Spioraid
and fógraíonn sé Dea Nuacht don domhan;
guimíd go dtabharfaidh an Spioraid riméad
do dhaoine atá faoi bhrón
agus dóchas dóibh siúd atá cráite
agus misneach dóibh siúd a bhfuil eagla orthu.
A Thiarna éist linn.

Leicseanár

Tagann gach ministéir i dtreo an tsagairt, duine ar dhuine
agus beireann sé/sí greim ar an leicseanár.
Sagart: Glac an leabhar ina bhfuil an Briathar atá tú le fógairt;
déan é a thaisceadh i do chroí; tabhair onóir dó i do shaol.
Freagra: Amen. *(tabhair an leicseanár don sagart)*

Beannú na Ministéirí

Sagart: Go mbeannaí Dia an tAthair sibh in bhúr ministreacht.
Go labhraí Dia an Mac a Dhea Nuacht tríbh.
Go maire Dia an Naomh Spiorad i ngach duine a chloiseann
sibh.
Freagra: Amen.

Admháil Chreidimh

Sagart: Fógraímís go léir le chéile ár gcreideamh,
a thugann dóchas dúinn agus a mhúsclaíonn sinn chun grá.
Pobal: Glór don Athair and don Mhac agus don Spiorad Naomh,
mar a bhí ar dtúis, mar atá anois agus mar a bhéas go bráth, le
saol na saol. Amen.

Filleann na ministéirí chuig a suíocháin.

CHAPTER 19

Justice Ministry in the Parish

Areas such as youth ministry, liturgy, communications, outreach come up again and again in parish renewal. Only rarely does the theme of justice surface. When it does, it often takes the shape of a justice group that engages in some particular initiative. Even then, an underlying question may still remain unexplored. What has 'justice' to do with the parish in the first place?

The meaning of the word

This lack of attention is out of step with the prominence the theme has assumed in church discourse and theology over recent decades. Since the advent of liberation theology in the late 1960s, action for justice has come to be highlighted more and more as a constitutive and indispensable expression of Christian faith.

The discrepancy is partly to do with our understanding of what 'justice' means. In common usage justice is about being fair. We talk, for example, of a just wage or of unjust discrimination. We talk about how fairly individuals and groups are treated. Justice also has strong legal connotations. We have the 'chief justice' in the courts, which themselves are about 'justice being done'. We have the image of the scales of justice. It is hard to see much in all this for the parish to take up.

In church usage charity is a far more familiar term than justice, and easier to apply to a parish context. But this has been changing significantly over the last century. Where church documents previously spoke of charity to the poor, they now speak of this as a question of justice. Charity connoted something very commendable but also somewhat optional. The shift to justice language brings obligation and urgency to the fore.

There is more to justice as a parish issue than we might have realised up till now. Christianity offers a vision of 'justice' that is rich and challenging. This vision puts us in touch with the fundamentals of what we believe and has the potential to transform how we understand parish.

Faith and justice

One of the deepest and most central insights of the Bible is that faith and justice are so intimately linked as to be inseparable. We may find this hard to get hold of. Faith, we think, is about God; justice is something to do with society. Yet Jeremiah has God saying about the practice of justice: *'Is this not to know me?'* (22:16). In God's eyes, practising justice *is* knowing God. Practising justice *is* faith.

The ten commandments, so familiar to us, are in fact all about this. Three commandments speak about our relationship to God – having no other gods, not taking God's name in vain, honouring the Sabbath. The remaining commandments speak about relations among God's people themselves – honouring parents, not killing or stealing or bearing false witness, not coveting, not being unfaithful.

The whole thrust of the commandments is that 'you can't have one without the other'! If we are not in right relation with one another as God's people, then we are not in right relation with God. Our faithfulness to God is reflected in and measured by the quality of our faithfulness to one another.

The talk of the Old Testament prophets is absorbed with this concern. They are scandalised by the separation of faith from justice. They see piety practised alongside oppression. Prayer and fasting on the one hand; unfeeling about the hungry and homeless on the other. They mourn that faith has come to this (see for instance Isaiah 58).

God-talk

All this has huge implications. It means that 'God-talk' is not to be identified with 'religious' talk and religious language. God-talk is justice talk, because justice is God's own talk, the preoccupation of God's heart. This is expressed vividly in Jesus' words: 'Just as you did it to one of the least of these who are members of my family you did it to me' (Matthew 25:40).

This brings us to the heart of the Christian meaning of justice. Justice is about God's dream for God's people. It is not primarily about being fair or any of that. It is something that God does, not us. Or more accurately, it is first of all something that God does, into which we as God's people are then drawn.

St Paul uses the word 'justification' for God's doing of justice. Justification is what God is doing in the world. It is God's activity of making us just, making us right, bringing us into right relationship with God. (The Old Testament speaks of 'righteousness'.) This is the activity that brought Israel out of exile in Egypt. It is the divine activity that is forever leading us from alienation into intimacy with God. It has its supreme and definitive expression in the cross and resurrection of Jesus, whom St Paul calls the righteousness of God (1 Corinthians 1:30).

When God's dream becomes a reality, we have what Jesus called 'the kingdom of God'. This is not just our final state of being ('heaven'). It is also already happening. Whenever there is right relationship with one another, there is the peace of God's kingdom, because that is what God passionately wants for God's people.

The prophets use a striking metaphor here, that of water. For instance, Amos says, 'Let justice roll down like waters and righteousness like an everflowing stream' (5:24). We all know how water gets in everywhere. Likewise every aspect of the life of God's people is meant to be permeated with God's justice. Justice is about the whole quality of life in the community.

Compassion

But society, as we know, can be very water-resistant, impermeable! We are appallingly numb to the pain that is around us. We seem to have managed to accommodate ourselves to living comfortably alongside all kinds of anguish and agony. It seems that

society has always been so. Even religious society; we have practised piety and remained numb.

There is a thread of something alternative right back in the
beginnings of our Jewish heritage. The detailed elaboration of
the ten commandments shows a particular regard for the defenceless – for the widow and the orphan, for the stranger and
for the slave. This regard reflects an almost unparalleled thirst
for justice at the time. It reflects a sense of scandal about hardship, that it is a negation of God's own thirst for rightness
among all God's people.

In Jesus this thread is dominant. It takes the form of compassion, the opposite of numbness. We see Jesus feeling 'compassion' towards the widow of Nain (Luke 7:13). We hear him extol
compassion in the figures of the Good Samaritan, who is 'moved
with compassion' for the man beaten by robbers, and of the
father who is 'filled with compassion' at the sight of his prodigal
son coming home (Luke 10:33; 15:20)

The way one writer put it is that in Jesus, as with the
prophets before him, 'the ache of God penetrates the numbness
of history'. Compassion feels the situation and pain of the other
as if it were one's own. But ultimately compassion is feeling
God's own feelings. It is caught up in God's own passion for
rightness – God's justice. It takes this kind of passion to pene-
trate through the numbness and to take the pain seriously. It has
become familiar to us as 'the passion of Jesus'.

Judgement
Justice is also linked to 'judgement', in this case the judgement
of God. But God's judgement is not the crippling burden our
spirituality has thought it to be. God's judgement is God's wrath
over the numbness and the lack of compassion in the world. It is
God's solidarity with the defenceless. It is God's promise of vin-
dication.

It is not enough to feel compassion. God's justice is both compassion and anger. To practise God's justice is also to ask why
the hurt happens, why the numbness goes on. Justice goes be-

yond 'tending the wounds'. Compassion begets criticism, as it demands that things be set 'right'.

A spirituality

The ongoing tension between compassion and numbness is reflected in the Old Testament institution of the 'sabbatical year' and the 'jubilee year'. These were special times of grace and favour when debts would be cancelled, slaves would be freed, soil would be left fallow, ancestral land would be restored. It would seem that the people recognised the need for a periodic cleaning out and a correcting of the inequalities that, like a weed, keep growing back up again.

It is the reason given that is key. In urging this liberality in relation to slaves, the text goes on, 'Remember that you were a slave in the land of Egypt and the Lord your God redeemed you; for this reason I lay this command upon you today' (Deuteronomy 15:15). Remembering our own alienation and justification, our own lostness and liberation, contains the secret of community living.

It could be summed up like this: 'Treat others as God has treated you; treat others as God would treat them.' That is justice – compassionate, inclusive, all-embracing, boundary-breaking. It is no less than a spirituality, a way of being that reaches into God. In the view of the scriptures it is no less than the path of holiness. 'Is this not to know me, says the Lord?'

In the parish

The above reflections allow us to see how justice ministry is meant to be at the heart of the life of the faith community. It is not 'ministry' in the sense of something that some people in the parish do for the sake of others, though that is part of it. It is a ministry that engages all of us. It is part of the definition of a 'ministering community'.

Today we are learning to use the words 'justice' and 'holiness' together. Holiness is practised in many ways. Mystical experience takes different forms. Today we see that there is a mystical experience in the practice of justice. The face of God is encountered therein. Justice is a spirituality. It is about how to be holy.

From this perspective we can think in new ways about the faith community as a community that is striving for holiness. Not in the sense of religious practices, though that is no less a part of it. But in the sense of the community connecting with God's own passion and becoming caught up in that passion. Put another way, there are new vistas opening up here on what it means to be a 'practising Catholic'. And this is what justice ministry in the parish is first and foremost about.

Young people

I think of young people immediately in this context. Many feel that it is young people especially who 'hold' this spirituality within the faith community. They have an intuition about justice that challenges the rest of us. They are alive to it when many others may be confined in their piety.

There is so much good news here, much of it coming from school-based initiatives. Young people fasting. Young people fundraising – for the homeless; for the developing world; in response to tragedy. The good news is about a responsiveness to need and to injustice. It is about an alertness and a willingness that witnesses.

We might see the parish as a place where justice ministry and youth ministry meet. The parish will have no trouble identifying a justice theme, whether in the developing world or nearer to home. Ideally it would have both dimensions, 'local and global'. And the parish will have no trouble finding young people who are enthusiastic to engage.

Already and not yet

It is not as if there is nothing already going on. In fact there are a number of ways in which justice ministry is already at work in the parish. It is just that we are not used to describing it in that language.

The work of the Vincent de Paul Society is about God's compassion penetrating through society's numbness. The support given by parish bereavement groups reflects God's own regard for the defenceless. Twinning with a developing world parish is an echo of Jesus' 'option for the poor'. Previously we might have thought of all this as 'charity'. Now we can appreciate it as the practice of justice.

There is more to it still. It is not just that small groups in the parish are engaged in this way. The financial support for V de P, for Trócaire, for humanitarian crises, is a statement of the huge regard in which people hold this work. It is an indication of the justice spirituality which is already alive in the faith community.

At the same time there is a long way to go. In the first chapter I spoke about the 'thrown together' nature of the parish. It is the collection of people who just happen to make up this particular faith community. They are rich and poor. They are people on the way up and people on the way down. They are settled and traveller. They are native and immigrant.

We may be thrown together, but to a large extent we do not or will not or cannot live together. Where a justice spirituality would experience God in the face of this other, we more often experience fear. Rich and poor, settled and traveller, native and immigrant; physically proximate, mentally and emotionally remote. God's justice, like water, needs to seep through our impervious hearts.

Background and foreground

John Paul II speaks about 'solidarity', a word which captures well the biblical and Christian vision of justice:

> 'Solidarity is not a feeling of vague compassion or shallow distress at the misfortunes of so many people both near and far. It is a firm and persevering determination to commit oneself to the common good, to the good of all and of each individual, because we are all really responsible for all.'

This is the spirituality that invites us all. But maybe in the process there is a rebalancing needed in our outlook. Maybe we see the Eucharist at the centre of the faith community and this kind of action nearer the circumference? Maybe parish is mainly about going to Mass and only secondly about justice? Maybe we need to rethink?

We might begin to consider solidarity as being in the foreground of the life of the faith community. Our main action in the world is our practising God's justice. The parish is there to enable us. It is there to resource us, so that we may more effectively be this presence of God's passion in the world. In a sense, Eucharist is in the background. It sends us forth to be the bread of life. It is not complete in itself.

If the parish sets up a justice group, all this is its agenda, awesome as it is. But it is necessary to enter into the bigger picture and to connect with its vision. For it is this vision which gives specific initiatives their overarching focus and their underlying depth.

CHAPTER 20

Communication

We are growing more and more to appreciate communication as a theme in the life of the faith community. The communications culture we live in makes the theme important. But that is not the only reason. Ultimately it is because Christianity itself is at its heart about communication.

Some parishes have taken action by putting a special group in place to address the theme. Other parishes have taken particular initiatives. But communication is bigger than any of that. It really is a concern and a dimension of every parish activity. The following reflections are in the form of a gradual unpacking of what the theme of communication includes.

A starting point

As a starting point, take a parish where there is little happening by way of parish renewal. Even there communications is prominent, as we can see by listing some activities that you would expect to find in any parish.

There is the homily on Sunday, which significantly shapes our whole experience of Mass. There are the notices or announcements at Mass. Like the homily they can be brief and to the point or they can go on and on. There are the church notice board and pamphlet stand. Sometimes they catch your attention, though often it looks as if the materials have been there forever. Then there is the parish school's religion teaching, a further exercise in communication.

Already we can see two aspects of communication. On the one hand, it is about media such as the notice board for getting information across. On the other, it is about the gospel, which it is our duty and commitment to share. And already, before we say anything about websites and the like, there is much to be done.

These basic forms of communication in the parish have the potential to greatly enhance the sense of welcome and belonging. Whether a major item like the homily or a less important one like the notice board, parish life could be transformed by a more deliberate attention to the quality of communication.

Creative innovations

These are just the basics you find in any parish. But many parishes have explored further and parish life has been enhanced by a range of new ideas. For instance, the parish may produce a newsletter or bulletin or information sheet. Some are short and simple, others are quite elaborate. Some are there simply to give information. Others are seen as part of the parish's effort to build community.

Many parishes have produced a parish brochure or parish directory, with lots of information about parish activities, perhaps also including a parish vision statement. All of it is intended as an invitation to people to belong and to participate. Often this production is combined with visiting newcomers to the parish. Some parishes distribute a special magazine, perhaps at Christmas celebrating their identity. Many distribute specially produced cards for Christmas and Easter.

The radio transmission of parish Mass for the housebound is a hugely appreciated development. The parish website has enabled a new form of engagement with parish for many people both near and far. Collecting parishioners' email addresses makes for a new way of communicating information and news. A parish bookstall or book and video library provides opportunities for people to deepen their knowledge.

Simply listing all these innovations helps us see that a great part of parish life is about communication and that attention to communication has the potential to greatly enhance the experience of faith community. It is about far more than disseminating

information. It is about the need to reach out. It is about the intuition that welcome and belonging are key and that they depend
on communication.

Ownership

A parish with many of these activities would have a lot going for
it. And yet there is more again involved in communication. The
theme is still opening up for us and we are still only beginning to
grasp its significance.

There can be surprisingly little awareness among parishioners generally of all that is going on in the parish. Even those
involved in parish groups surprise themselves when they make
a list of all that is going on! We say that knowledge is power;
participation implies information. If people are to have a sense
of ownership they need to have a familiarity with and an interest in what happens in their own parish. Communication is a
huge part of creating a sense of a people's parish, in contrast to a
sense of parish as something that somebody else runs for my
benefit.

Again, despite all that may be going on, parish groups know
very little about each other. Each is busy with its own patch.
They know little about what other groups are up to. They may
not know the people in the other groups. There is a the need for
cohesiveness, for all to feel that they are all working from the
same script and towards the same vision, and for all to appreciate how their 'bit' fits into an overall picture.

Here again communication is the issue. An initiative such as
a parish open day has a role here. Not only do parishioners get
to see what goes on in the different groups. The groups themselves get to know one another. Links are made and everybody
gets a boost simply from getting to know other parish workers.
But the pastoral council also has a role. It has the main responsibility for developing cohesiveness. That begins by developing
positive relationships with all the groups in the parish.

A related communications issue concerns the profile of the
pastoral council in the parish. It is sobering to realise how little is

known about most councils. They were not set up in secret, yet it is as if they did not exist. At most, people have a vague idea that there is something there, but little sense of what it actually does. Again it is about ownership. If people are to feel that it is their pastoral council there needs to be a quality communication between the council and the parish at large.

Needs and gifts

Unpacking the communications theme, we find that there is yet more to be explored. Most of what has been listed above is about what goes from the 'parish' out to its people. But communication is two-way. It is also about listening.

The existence of many parish groups can deceive people into thinking that everything is being catered for. The feedback from a parish assembly can tempt people to think that they now know the needs. But the people at the assembly and the people in the groups are a small fraction of the faith community. We are only in touch with the real needs when God's people have articulated their own needs.

This demands two-way communication. The challenge of communication is a challenge to listen, to find creative ways of listening, of 'hearing into speech' the silent and submerged voices, the unspoken needs. Otherwise we remain in a presuming and providing mode, presuming to know what people need and then providing for them. When people are asked what they want, they are also being invited into ownership.

Discovering needs and discovering gifts are intimately related. There are great gifts in the faith community that nobody knows about, even the people themselves. Communication is also about recognising the gifts, affirming them, inviting them forth. Ministry can usefully be seen in terms of a communications process that matches gifts to needs, where people are delighted to become involved when they realise that their gift responds to a felt need.

Here more than anywhere we realise that the most powerful communication is face-to-face. Gifts and needs come to light when one person notices another, asks another, encourages another. This is the kind of evangelisation every parishioner can participate in. In the process they are once again assuming ownership. Parish leadership groups and parish communication groups have a big role to play in encouraging this kind of one-to-one interaction.

Who we are

A further dimension of parish communication takes in the theme of change. In the parish, like everywhere else, communication is vital in managing change. It seeks to keep everybody 'onside'. It seeks to be inclusive. It seeks to accommodate all. It devotes time to conversation, where people have the chance to tease out and come to terms with what is dying and what is being born in our experience of church.

In a time of change there is a greater need to communicate who we are and the good news that fills our hearts. When we think of all those baptised people who partake only at the fringes, we know that there are so many people in the parish who have never experienced what Christian community can be like. And if we do not communicate they will never know. We have to put ourselves forward.

In communicating who we are, we also know that we would describe ourselves differently today than we would have in the past. The gospel is the same, but our experience of church has moved on. Many who have ceased to participate do not know this. Many who still participate have not come to terms with the change. There is a huge need for the kind of conversations that can help us articulate who we are in a new situation. They are central to any outreach.

Finally, a new model of parish has meant a new relationship between clergy and laity, characterised by equality, partnership and ownership. This too demands a quality communication. It demands an openness and transparency about how decisions are made. It demands a commitment to being consultative and accountable to one another. It highlights that 'how' we communicate is as important as 'what' we say.

Functions of communication

It is clear that communications is pivotal. We are only beginning to scratch the surface. We are only beginning to grasp the link between communication and faith community. Somebody I know put it like this: Is it *only* communication that builds community?

We might have thought of communication as just one aspect. We might have thought of a communications group alongside the liturgy group, the bereavement group, the finance group. But perhaps communication is at the heart of what every group is doing? Perhaps it is at the heart of what every 'practising' Christian is doing?

I have listed a huge range of activities that revolve around communication – the minimal communication that goes on in the dormant parish; the life-giving new initiatives being taken on in more and more parishes; the communication challenges that still draw us forward. From this list a number of functions of communication can be pinpointed.

Communication has an *ownership* function. Sharing information and sharing experiences creates awareness and interest. It creates a sense of participation and involvement and ownership. It builds a shared vision.

It has a *community building* function. Much communication is an effort to create a feeling of welcome and belonging. It is an outreach in words and actions that says to people: 'We notice that you are there; we care that you exist; we regard you with respect; we cherish you as one of us.'

It has a function of *breaking silence*. Many needs are hidden and do not protest themselves. Many gifts are submerged and do not assert themselves. But communication listens and 'hears into speech'. It asks the needs to name themselves. It invites the gifts to reveal themselves.

It has a *witnessing* function. We communicate in order to share who we are, because what we are is not something to be hoarded or hidden, but something that propels us outwards. Most of this witness is in our action, some of it in our words. It is the quality of our presence, offering suggestive, refreshing ideas about what being a Christian might mean.

And it has a function of *proclaiming good news*. What is common to all the examples of communication above is that they are all meant to be an experience of hearing good news. Whether it is the homily, the newsletter or the assembly; whether it is identifying needs or managing change; whether it is the notice board or the website; if it is not an experience of hearing good news, of being welcomed by good news, it is nothing.

Christianity and communication

This suggests a theological reflection. Is not Christianity itself at heart about communication and nothing else? It is the story of God entering into dialogue with humanity. It is a conversation between God and humanity, stretching through history, culminating in the Incarnation. God and humanity – reaching out, speaking, listening, understanding and misunderstanding, getting the point, losing the plot, falling out, growing closer.

The divine conversation continues in and through our human conversations. God depends on our communicating if God's love is to be known in the world. St Paul has given us the sharpest expression of this:

> 'How are they to call on one in whom they have not believed? And how are they to believe in one of whom they have never heard? And how are they to hear without someone to proclaim him? And how are they to proclaim him unless they are sent? As it is written, How beautiful are the feet of those who bring good news!' (Romans 10:14-15).

If there is no communication there is no Christianity. If there is no communication there is no faith community. More communication means more faith community. Communication is the energy in who we are. It creates the forum wherein the Spirit works.

A communications group

The above gives an agenda, not just for a communications

group, but for a parish. It would not make sense simply to leave all this to a particular group. It is a parish-wide agenda. In driving this agenda, it makes sense for the pastoral council to assume a central role, in collaboration with the communications group.

For the communications group itself, since the agenda is so great, perhaps the place to start might be to initiate itself into the rich meanings contained in the theme. This would give a shape and a vision to whatever initiatives follow. It would be a reference point as the work proceeds.

As regards an actual agenda of work, each parish will read the above list of possibilities and challenges differently, according to its particular circumstances. The homily, naming needs, radio Mass, welcoming newcomers, website, open days, parish library, newsletter, and so on. No one can say, except the parish itself, how to proceed.

Perhaps the 'functions of communication' listed above might provide a guideline. When the parish has a broad vision of what communication means within the life of the parish; when it has given expression to this in a 'communications dream' for the parish; then it will be proceeding with a strong sense of direction.

CHAPTER 21

The Parish and Young People

'Youth' may be the most often repeated word at parish meetings. It comes up with numbing predictability. Often there is an air of frustration and helplessness. Often it is confused as to what exactly people want. All in all it seems to be the most difficult single issue on the parish agenda.

This chapter has a modest intention. It asks the question: what is the particular niche of the parish when it comes to youth ministry? I propose that the parish cannot do everything and that the way forward is to get clear about the specific 'something' that the parish can do, its own distinctive connection with young people.

Background

By way of background, it might be worth going over a few distinctions, though they will be familiar to those ministering in this area. First of all, we speak of youth ministry where we would previously have spoken of youth work. 'Youth ministry' has an eye to the faith of young people. 'Youth work' addresses the young person's recreational, personal and social development.

The two cannot be divorced, but faith has been the focus of most church workers in recent times. At the same time, this is far from meaning that youth ministry is about getting young people to go to Mass. In fact the experience of young people has much to teach the faith community today about the meaning of faith itself.

Secondly, the term 'young people' has grown elastic. In recent practice the term has stretched in one direction to include young adults, say up to the mid-20s or so. And it has stretched in the other direction to embrace children, even as young as first communion age. In the latter case, the thinking is that starting in the teens is already too late, that the foundation has to be laid much earlier.

Thirdly, with reference to teenagers specifically, there has been a pattern of moving away from the parish towards the school as a base for youth ministry. Those working in youth ministry observe that it is difficult to establish lines of contact with these young people in the parish, whereas there is a readily accessible clientele in the second-level school. From that base they can then work to build up links with the local parishes.

The niche of the parish
This last point leads into what seems to me to be a key statement. Youth ministry is not the sole job of the parish. In the teenage years a lot of very good ministry to young people happens in the context of the school. This includes formal religious education, prayer formation, retreats, spiritual accompaniment, opportunities for social justice involvement.

In addition, a lot of youth ministry happens in a trans-parish context, particularly through the initiative of diocesan youth agencies. For instance, there are pilgrimages for young people to such centres as Lourdes and Santiago di Campostella. There is leadership training for young people, such as the *Meitheal* and *Anois* programmes. There is now formal professional training available for people engaged in youth ministry.

Youth ministry, then, is bigger than the parish. There are other major players. It may be that the parish is not the main player. At least it is but one piece of a larger jigsaw. Perhaps the school should be recognised as the central base. Perhaps also it is a fact that, as one worker put it, youth ministry in the parish is doomed without a diocesan policy.

These perspectives clear the way for asking: if youth ministry is bigger than the parish, and if the parish is one of a number of players, what then is the distinctive niche of the parish? Given that it cannot do everything, what can it do? What is its particular – distinctive, but modest – contribution? What can it offer that nobody else can?

Laying foundations

The first answer to this question is to highlight the immense contribution the parish can and does make at the initial point of youth ministry, namely, the primary school stage. I am thinking particularly of preparation programmes for first communion and confirmation, as well as of the family Mass. Where these are happening in earnest, they are among the most significant and life-giving enterprises in parish life.

The youth ministry done at this stage is laying a foundation for everything that follows. It is giving boys and girls a warm, positive, enriching experience of faith community. It is affirming families in a deep way and creating a space for them to celebrate the God who is already there in their homes. It is supporting families as primary agents of youth ministry.

Some parishes have been working hard at laying this foundation and want to know how to build on it in the teenage years. But others are worrying about the next stage before they have attended sufficiently to the foundations. It is like starting the building on the second storey.

For the parish, youth ministry begins at primary school level. There should be no apology about seeing this as youth ministry in its foundational stage. What the parish does here is the core of its distinctive contribution to young people, a contribution that nobody else can emulate.

Principles and perspectives

Speaking of the next, teenage stage, one parish worker suggested as follows: we do a lot at the primary school stage, they'll come back to us when they're marrying and having children, so maybe just let them to themselves in the in-between time when church is the least of their interests. It was said tongue in cheek. At the same time it does capture something, namely, that our expectations should be realistic as regards teenage youth ministry in the parish.

The following are some perspectives that might guide the exploration. Firstly, ministry to young people should be the same as ministry to any people, a ministry of welcome and belonging. Whatever is done should have this central aspiration, that young people experience the parish as a place where they are welcome, accepted as they are and cherished for who they are.

Here there is no intent to convert or 'bring back'. It is simply, how do we communicate welcome? Just as we are eco-friendly and wheelchair-friendly and family-friendly, so we seek to be youth-friendly. For instance, if there were one Mass at the weekend that was a youth-friendly liturgy, integrating young people's thinking and language and music, that in itself would be a huge statement of welcome.

Secondly, young people like all people should experience the parish as a place where they are cared for, where they hear the message: 'We care that you exist.' It should be clear to young people that the parish is a place that has some appreciation for what it is like to be a young person and for what troubles young people. The special Masses at exam time work better in some cases than in others, but they suggest that gestures expressing care can be significant.

Thirdly, youth ministry is also family ministry. The young person is not an isolated individual. He or she is a member of a family, a person for whom family remains very important. Ongoing attention to the family on the part of the parish is implicitly youth ministry also. It is enabling the family to be a place where young people feel ministered to and called to ministry. The post-confirmation GIFT programme is a reminder of the family dimension of youth ministry.

Fourthly, the 'face' of faith for young people is not going to Mass. Faith for them is justice and service. In this young people have a clear intuition as to the profound link between faith and justice that is distinctive of Judaeo-Christian religion. Initiatives that afford young people the opportunity to serve are resonating deeply with their own sense of things. A 'junior' Vincent de Paul conference or twinning with a parish in the developing world or a Christmas fast are examples of the kind of project that can engage young people deeply.

Fifthly, youth ministry is not one-way. It is 'for' young people; it is 'with' young people; but it is also *by* young people. Young people are agents and not just recipients. They have an active role in ministering to one another. As the justice theme in the last paragraph illustrates, they have a role in ministering to adults also as they bring a new richness to how faith is understood and practised in the community.

If young people are also leaders, that suggests a style of youth ministry that invites young people in as active partners from the start. In a partnership of young people and (suitable) older people, young people's experience and perceptions are valued. They find space to articulate their own needs as well as to respond openly to proposals. In that approach, any initiatives that emerge will more likely be owned and embraced by young people themselves.

Such an approach might conceivably lead to some parallel form of pastoral council for young people specifically. Most parishes find it hard enough to achieve an adequate representation of people in their thirties and forties on the pastoral council. Many would acknowledge that young people might have more energy for a forum comprised of their peers than one where they are just one or two among a 'crowd of oul' ones'!

Challenge to the parish

A major part of the challenge to the parish in all this is to get its own thinking right. As I said the issue of 'youth' comes up with boring inevitability in parish discussions. But there is much confused thinking. A typical meeting, for instance, would have one person going on about no young people at Mass, to be followed by another who praises the virtues of young people today. It makes you wonder: just where is the problem?

One thread in this is what I might describe as a self-centred concern among some parishioners. I am thinking of churchgoers who are by and large happy with the parish as it is (some would prefer it as it was). They wonder: why can't young people come back? I recall years ago one such parishioner complaining, 'we weren't allowed to be bored at Mass'! There is anger here, as well as sadness on the part of older people, that young people do not share their experience of church.

Yet, this way of thinking is saying to young people, 'you come into our church as it is'. There is no sense of accommodating that church to the experience of young people. That would disturb the peace, with all the noise and God knows what else young people would bring with them. There is no listening in this, nor any interest in being challenged. It is on our terms only.

More and more people now see that the only youth ministry that has any hope of bearing fruit is that which is done out of a positive disposition. Young people are as wonderful and as vulnerable as anybody else. They have a huge amount to teach older people. They have huge potential to revitalise the faith community. They are welcome.

A young face to parish ministry
Another part of the challenge to the parish is to radically review the age profile of those who are involved in the parish. There needs to be a 'preferential option' for young people right across parish ministries. I am thinking of one parish which, when setting up a parish council, required that half the members must be under forty; otherwise it would not go ahead.

What I am thinking is that an option for young people is not just about putting youth ministry high on the parish agenda. It is also about attaining a youth profile in parish ministries – 'youth' in the sense of young adults. Without any belittling of what older people bring to parish ministry, there is no doubt that where younger adults are seen to be involved, it brings a sense of life and energy that is incomparable.

It is easier said than done, but maybe we let ourselves off the hook too easily. We try and get no response and resign ourselves to failure. But maybe the recruiting stage does not get the time and concentration it requires? Maybe we should say that we are going to give ourselves time to find younger people – lots of time – and that we are not going to proceed until we find them.

Where to start?

The first thing to do might be for a group of people to gather and talk through how they see young people. But not just anybody. It is probably unrealistic to presume that everybody will have the same positive perspective that is necessary for this kind of ministry.

The group that emerges would do well to think through some of the basic questions touched on here. How do we see youth ministry in our parish? What is its purpose, its goal? Many of us want to do something but are confused about the why. We come with different objectives in mind. We need a vision that is about far more than getting young people back to Mass.

From here the group can go on to identify the core contribution they feel the parish can make to the life and faith of the young person. A parish dream for youth ministry might be composed. This could be the inspiration and the reference point for subsequent policy and planning.

It is critical to invite young persons themselves into the process at an early stage. Those who come to Mass might be invited, or those who were involved in the parish at a younger age. A link could be made with the local second-level school. If young people join the process they join as equals. They are going to be partners with adults in leading the parish's youth ministry.

A youth worker?

Where parishes invest in professional lay ministry, they most frequently look for somebody who can work in youth ministry. A parish might do this on its own or together with neighbouring parishes. But such an initiative should not substitute for thinking and planning on the part of the parish. Unfortunately it sometimes does.

Most parishes do not know what to do when it comes to youth ministry. They are not even sure what they want. It is unsatisfactory for the parish to expect a youth minister or youth worker to provide for this gap. It is like saying to them: 'We don't know exactly what we want you to do, but we want you to do it.'

The parish itself needs to think through the basic questions and to formulate what it wants. Then it can say to the youth minister: 'This is our plan; this is our brief for you.' They can then dialogue and modify the brief in the light of the wisdom and expertise that this particular worker brings.

CHAPTER 22

Visiting in the Parish

A great intuition of people involved in parishes today is that hospitality is at the heart of renewal and revitalisation. Setting up a visiting team is a practical way of expressing this spirit of hospitality and many parishes are finding it to be a most rewarding and creative project. Usually parishioners would visit in pairs, aiming to cover either the whole parish or a section of it.

Visiting is an unusual form of hospitality. We would associate hospitality with receiving visitors or welcoming people to our place. In this case we are going to people in their place, hoping for their welcome, in order to communicate something of our sense of the parish as a welcoming, embracing community of faith. Welcome is not just something offered to those who come our way. It is the spirit in which we reach out.

Visiting illustrates a particular form of evangelisation. In today's parish innovative strategies are needed in reaching out with the good news. But a large part of evangelisation is about doing familiar things in a new way. Such is the case with baptisms, with first communion and confirmation, with weddings and funerals. Such is the case with visitation, which traditionally has been a staple part of the ministry exercised by the priest on his own.

What follows is the outline of a training programme for a visiting team. Experience indicates that the fruitfulness of a visiting project multiplies when there is careful preparation. In particular, its success depends on getting clear about why this project is being taken up and on the team having a clear and inspiring sense of purpose about what they are doing.

Why visit?

It is striking that at a time when people's dwellings are becoming more private – epitomised by the apartment block – parishes are becoming more rather than less interested in visiting. But it is crucial for the parish to clarify its motivation. It is too easy to skim over this question and to be satisfied with 'it sounds like a good idea; let's do it'. And off the visitors go, armed perhaps with the new parish directory, not really clear about why they are visiting.

In the process, different motives are at work in the visiting team. It may be seen as a befriending exercise, reaching out in friendship. It may have a somewhat judgemental tone, wanting people to go back to Mass. It may have a utilitarian motive, done to gather information, for instance with the help of a questionnaire. It may be evangelistic in tone, the gospel very much up front. It may be seen as a communications initiative, designed to project something of what we are at in our parish.

I think the core potential of a visiting project lies in its being a powerful statement of who we are. I concluded the first chapter above by speaking of the very existence of the parish as an assurance of care for each individual within its boundaries. There is possibly no expression of this care that is more tangible than calling on people's doors with a friendly 'hello'.

In a simple act, visiting expresses very eloquently that we aspire to be welcoming, inclusive, non-judgemental and that this is what the gospel is about. This eloquent statement is itself the evangelisation. There may be follow-up planned. There will be spin-offs, new needs uncovered, new people involved. But there is no ulterior motive. The visiting is not a means to an end. It itself is the end; it itself is the communication of good news.

This will be an important point for those who might become involved on the team. They will be relieved and encouraged to know that the core action is the familiar, ordinary human action of reaching out to others in a friendly spirit. Generally they would not see themselves as bringing a 'religious' message or as competent to talk about 'religion'. But they would see themselves, as up-front members of the faith community, chatting in a warm friendly way with other parishioners.

Why training?

A course of training sessions does great things for the people on the visiting team. While their consent to join the team indicates their interest and willingness, this will be mixed with a sense of apprehension. The sessions ease this through the bonding experienced in the team. People grow more confident. They get a feeling of 'we can do this' and the course ends with their enthusiasm increasing.

The training also addresses the central question stressed above, that of the 'why?' Attention to this brings a clarity of purpose. The team becomes clear about what it is and what it is not about. There is now a strong likelihood that all will be 'singing from the same hymn sheet'.

In what follows I will give the outline of six training sessions. The themes are: 'Introductions'; 'Reflecting on parish'; 'On the doorstep'; 'Role-play'; 'Listening'; 'Practicalities'. In addition, there are outlines of a preparatory meeting and of a post-visiting reflection. Each session lasts for about an hour and a quarter.

The number of sessions is not set in stone. The course can be shortened, though I think that five or six sessions is the best. It takes that kind of time to build up the group and to get through the themes that deserve attention. The parish might even opt to have more than six sessions, or to add an evening or afternoon of prayer at the end of the training.

Preparatory meeting

First there is a meeting or a series of meetings of those who are heading up the project. They may be the pastoral council or a group from the council or a separate team. The person(s) to present the course may be from this group or an outside facilitator may be taken on board.

This group needs, first of all, to clarify the purpose of the visiting. One could, of course, leave it to the team of visitors to determine the purpose. But I think it is fairer and wiser for the organising team to formulate the purpose and then to present it to the visiting team. The latter can still have an input but they will appreciate the offer of direction. Defining the purpose will also include any follow-up that may be envisaged.

Next the group has to decide the scale of the project. Are we going to visit the whole parish? Are we going to visit just a section for now? How long does a typical visit last? In what period of time do we want to complete the visiting? What size of team does this require? Regarding the numbers required, people tend to prefer to visit in pairs, as it helps with confidence. Others, though, would feel that visiting singly is better, as it means that you are approaching people in weakness rather than strength.

From this a timescale can be drafted, with a recruiting stage, a training stage and a visiting stage. The recruiting has to be negotiated carefully; not all who are interested would be suitable. Something other than an open invitation is needed. Those at the preparatory meeting, and perhaps other parish groups also, might be invited to submit nominations. Then a small group might finalise the list of those to be invited. Nominees who are not selected might be involved in the more administrative aspects of the project.

Introductions (Session one)
The first session for the team of visitors is largely about 'getting-to-know-you'. For instance, ask the group to form pairs with people who do not know each other. Say who you are; share your hopes and fears for the visiting. Then join two pairs together; introduce your partner to the other pair; all four then discuss what they see as the reasons for this project.

As the groups feed back, people will be exposed to different perspectives. Most of the feedback will be around themes of building community, showing care and concern, welcome and friendship, listening to what people have to say about the parish, telling people about the parish. There may also be things to iron out. There may be a 'bring them back' thread in the feedback. There may be somebody with an overly 'religious' intent. But the feedback will by and large confirm the purposes already identified.

This might be followed by a little input on the significance of visiting teams as part of what John Paul II calls the 'new evangelisation' in today's church. This would help deepen people's sense of mission and motivation. Alternatively, people could go back into the groups with the question: 'What do you think we can realistically expect to achieve from this exercise?'

The meeting concludes with prayer, for instance the prayer 'Setting Out' in my *Prayer Reflections for Group Meetings* (all the prayer suggestions that follow are from the same source). The subsequent sessions will start with prayer and it will be a very important factor in the whole process. Finally, the presenter should write up the feedback about the reasons for visiting, to present back to the group at the next session.

Reflecting on parish (Session two)
The rest of the sessions will be very practical, so it is good to have one reflective session. Two possibilities are offered below. With a longer session it might be possible to address both. A suitable prayer to begin with would be 'What is a Parish for?'

The first possibility is an exercise reflecting on why people have fallen away from church participation. The purpose of this is to encourage a positive disposition towards those who will be visited. Many of them may be in this situation and it is crucial that they are approached in a friendly, respectful and hospitable manner.

The group is asked the question, 'Why do you think that people have stopped participating?' Ask people to think quietly, perhaps suggesting different categories – young and old, men and women, rich and poor. Then form into groups to pool the ideas, followed by feedback in the full group.

What emerges is a variety of different factors – people who have drifted; the pace of life; bad experiences of church; individualistic spirituality; peer pressure; church teachings; double standards; suffering and hardship. This variety should diffuse judgemental tendencies and make for an understanding disposition. It also makes it clear that the church itself bears some of the responsibility, so that we should be wary of simply trying to 'bring them back'.

The second possibility is an 'ideal parish' exercise, to build up a shared vision of parish to ground and inspire the group's outreach. It could begin with a quiet meditation. People reflect first on the parishes they have lived in, what moments and memories stand out. They then reflect on their experience of this parish, where they see themselves in the community, how they feel about the parish, what they would like to see happening in the parish.

They then share from this in groups, perhaps with a focusing sentence to complete, such as, 'Ideally, our parish is a place where…' (see the chapter above on vision statements for more alternatives). One would expect themes such as inclusiveness, people being cared for, equality and acceptance, community, a sense of God and a living liturgy to come up. There could well be material here to write up as a kind of vision statement to include with whatever is being distributed on the visits.

On the doorstep (Session three)

The third session is about what to say and do for those precious few minutes on the doorstep. The session might begin with the prayer 'Visiting in the Parish'. This should be followed with a handout and recap of the previous session. Then focus on the theme. On average there might be five or ten minutes on the doorstep. So it is important to get it right – and it is important that everybody is following much the same approach.

Begin with a 'buzz' period. Ask people to share in pairs on the basic message or impression they want to leave in those few minutes. Typical feedback would include: 'We're calling because we care'; 'You are important'; 'This is a caring parish'; 'The church welcomes you'. The contrast is immediately obvious with many who knock on our own door. In this case, we're not looking for your money. You are not being hooked. What you think matters to us.

This is followed by a handout which is a draft script for the time on the doorstep. People will divide into groups to discuss this, to add and to subtract. A refined script will then be submitted at a subsequent session and the group will finalise this as the 'hymn sheet' that all will sing from. It gets people focused, it gets them thinking and it allows them to shape for themselves what they are going to say.

The script offers a sequence of steps to go through and a text of what to say. This might be as follows: suggested introductory words (saying your name, etc); crisp explanatory text as to why you are there; offering a leaflet of some sort about the parish; asking the person if there is anything they would like to say; thanks, possible offer to call back.

The 'leaflet' could be a little brochure. It could be a parish directory. It could include some of the material from the training sessions. Having something like that gives the visitors a support to lean on, as well as a practical focus for conversation. The group might have further ideas on this and the actual leaflet or whatever can be developed in parallel with the training.

The session concludes with practical arrangements for the next session's role play (see below).

Role play (Session four)

This session is taken up with a number of short role-plays on visitation, plus reflection on the experience, with a view to extracting learnings about the 'do's and don'ts' of visiting. Begin with the prayer, 'A Prayer before Parish Visitation'.

At the previous session a number of volunteers (four should be ideal) will each have been given a short text about the role they are to adopt when being visited in the role-play. At the start of this session, four pairs will need to volunteer to be the visitors. These pairs will not know in advance what role is to be enacted when they call.

The roles should reflect something of the mix of situations

that are likely to arise. This will vary from parish to parish. For instance, one might be a middle-aged person who has experienced tragedy but who does not find it easy to talk. Another might be somebody who has drifted from church, polite but not really interested. There might be one that will generate a bit of humour, or one that takes the visitors by surprise (when the door opens they are confronted with an unstoppable talker or a born-again Christian).

After each 'act', ask the person to read out the role given to them. Wait until all are completed before processing. Ask people how they felt, both the visitors and those being visited. The 'audience' will readily join in. Although it is artificial there will be a tangible sense of what it will be like.

The discussion should lead into some learnings. For instance: don't pry; look interested; the pair support one another by alternating; don't argue. The group could be asked; what is the single insight or learning that you will take with you from this exercise?

Listening (Session five)

It will be clear at this stage that listening is at the heart of visiting. Therefore this session on listening will be building on what has gone before and focusing some of the learning. It might begin with the prayer 'A Listening Heart', which is also a meditation on our own personal experience of listening and being listened to.

The group would be put through one of the various listening exercises available (for instance, see those in *Parish Renewal, Volume 2,* edited Donal Harrington, page 84). Whatever exercise is chosen should give the individuals the chance to experience the challenge of listening properly, the joy of being listened to, the frustration of not being heard.

Processing of the exercise begins by asking people how they felt. As with the role play, there will be plenty of feedback. This can be guided gently in the direction of naming factors that make for good/bad listening – body language, eye contact, hear-

ing what is half said, not interrupting, not trying to solve problems, and so on. The group could be invited to formulate its 'ten
commandments' for listening. Or a handout listing key factors
could be distributed and discussed.

In preparation for the final session, the organising team or
the priest should be given a list of practical questions to do some
initial work on (see below). Of course, all could be given a copy
to be thinking about.

Practicalities (Session six)

The final session is mainly taken up with all the practical
arrangements. It begins with a prayer such as 'Christians are
Missionaries' or 'There is Enough'. This might appropriately be
followed by or combined with a little reflection, inviting partici-
pants to articulate how they have found the experience so far.
This could also have been done at one of the previous sessions,
but it is very worthwhile for the group to hear itself articulating
its own experience.

A sheet of practical questions to be addressed is handed out.
Somebody will have been working on these questions since the
previous session. That will not prevent the group having an
input, but it will speed things up a lot.

The sheet includes questions like: When do we start? What
day of the week / what time of day? How many visits per time?
Who makes out the list? What pairings? Will the pairings rotate?
Will people be notified that we're coming? If there's no answer,
do we revisit? Do we pray together before visiting? Do we meet
afterwards? How do we record and relay information? What
publicity in the parish? Will we be publicly 'commissioned'?

It could be useful to finish by reflecting on the question:
'What kind of outcome can we realistically expect?' (This might
have already come up in the first session.) While hopes and enthusiasm will be high at this stage, it will be worth getting across
both that this is not going to change the world and that it is
going to be a very significant event for the parish.

Review meeting

There may be a celebration to honour the completed experience. There should also be a review meeting, where the focus is on what the parish can learn from the venture. For this it might be appropriate that members of the pastoral council be present. The prayer 'Thanks for our Ministry' could be used, either at the start or the end of the meeting.

The meeting itself can be quite simple. First, invite the team of visitors to say what it was like for themselves individually and what stands out for them from the whole experience. They might do this in pairs before sharing in the larger group.

Second, initiate a discussion on what the parish should be hearing from this and what the parish could take forward. For example, some issue might have kept coming up again and again, such as loneliness or the needs of young families. Or some desire might have been expressed repeatedly, such as for a meeting place in the parish.

If something significant has surfaced, a group such as the pastoral council can then place it on its own agenda. Some of the visiting team might be interested in staying on for this follow through. Meanwhile, just as the project began with publicity in the parish, so it might conclude by announcing to the parish the outcomes of all the work put in.

CHAPTER 23

Mass Ministry

This chapter and the next – on the Sunday Eucharist and on caring ministries – take up again the foundational themes of the second chapter ('The Last Supper'), but this time from the perspective of specific areas of ministry in the parish.

Mass is people's main experience of 'church'. It is the only contact for many if not most people. Leave aside the very involved and think of those who just 'come to Mass'. It is the only 'church' bit in the week. A good few would be hard pressed to explain why they are there in the first place. For many of them 'regular' attendance has come to mean occasional rather than weekly. And outside of these there is a perhaps bigger group for whom church is quite marginal to their lives, who only pass through the doors for a funeral and at Christmas.

Taking all this into account it seems obvious that Mass should be the priority focus for time, energy and resources in the parish. So many people for whom it is the only point of contact. So many where it provides an opportunity for outreach without having to leave the building. In terms of strategy it would be incomprehensible not to target Mass in a major way.

But if Mass – particularly weekend Mass, funerals and Christmas – is to be central to pastoral strategy, there is one indispensable foundation. We ourselves must learn to view Mass differently. Making Mass central to planning is not about doing something with the Mass in order to make a certain impact on some of those present. Rather, it is about looking at Mass differently for ourselves.

In this sense 'outreach' is about 'inreach'. The starting point is our own experience. If we ourselves – meaning the familiar faces who regularly attend – transform our own way of seeing the Mass, then it will become a qualitatively different experience for us. And that is what will then be experienced by anybody who happens to be there.

Celebration

The term used by the first Christians was 'the breaking of bread' (e.g. Acts 2:42, 46). They did not 'go to Mass'. They gathered to break bread together. Eucharist was an action that the people did together. The action they did had a quality of remembering the one who said, 'do this [break bread] in memory of me'. And it had a quality of celebrating; it was a remembering that filled people's hearts with hope.

Even now, decades after Vatican II, we are still quite distanced from this sense of 'Mass'. We were conditioned to something else, over generations. We became habituated to 'getting' Mass or 'hearing' Mass. We thought in terms of our Sunday 'obligation', of Mass as a duty. We thought in terms of the minimum. You could not arrive any later than the creed if you were to fulfil your obligation. You could go the whole year without 'going to' communion (or even staying on for that part).

That culture is not stripped away easily. How far into the baptised community has it penetrated that we are all celebrants and that the priest 'presides'? How far has it penetrated that we not watching a show, that we are not fulfilling a duty, that we are not 'getting Mass in', that it is more than a routine?

Connecting

What is the key thing that should be happening any individual at any Mass? The best pastoral thinking today, I suggest, would say that 'connecting' is the most important thing happening. This theme has already come up in previous chapters. We have a huge need in our souls to connect faith and life, God and the ordinary, religion and the everyday. The sense of disconnection is widespread. 'Religion' and 'holiness' – even 'God' – seem to so many to be something so far away as to be irrelevant.

The Eucharist is meant to be a connecting. After all, the 'bread' that we break is about 'incarnation', the one we call 'God' taking an ordinary shape we can recognise. Just as God connects with humanity in Jesus, so the Eucharist is about God connecting with us. We bring our life – our feeling selves, our pounding hearts – into this sacred space. And we connect.

At least that is the theory. But as I approach the church, sometimes I have to leave my life at the door – my efforts, my tears, my loves, my failures, my desire. I know that it will not be 'taken up' into the sacred space. What goes on in there and what goes on in me are two different worlds and no connection will be made for me.

Sometimes, of course, it is I who fail to see the link. My daily life seems an ocean apart from this ritual. I cannot see how they might connect. Or maybe I am not even alive to the possibility of connecting. I am not even sure why I am here.

What is meant to happen, and what the 'Offertory' stands for, is that, as the gifts are brought up to the altar, I find myself called, addressed. I am not to watch this movement with gifts to the altar. I am to be part of it. As I am, my need and my joy, my light and my darkness. St Paul spoke of this 'offering' when he said to present our bodies as a living sacrifice (Romans 12:1).

We know from experience that the most relevant and meaningful Mass is the one where we ourselves are involved, for instance when somebody close is getting married or when a dear friend has died. There is no need for anybody to make a connection. The connection is there, it is alive. Our whole selves are engaged in this ritual. Our whole selves are on the altar.

St Augustine put it like this to those who had been baptised: 'It is your own mystery that has been placed on the table of the Lord.' He was not talking of special Masses, however. He was talking about each and every Eucharist. The mystery is not 'up there'. It incorporates us. When it does we are 'connected'.

The Body
There is a further dimension to this connecting. It is not just

making connection between my faith and my life. It is not just connecting between me and God. It is also our connecting with one another. Eucharist is very personal but it is not private. We do it together.

Vatican II saw that the greatest expression of 'church' is when we are all actively participating at the same Eucharist in one prayer, at one altar. This feeling of unity and solidarity is regularly missing. If there is more than one weekend Mass in the parish, we are never all together. In addition more and more people move around different churches at weekends.

More seriously, there is so often a sense that we are more a chance collection of individuals than a community. This is intensified by our tendency towards a privatised spirituality. In the past people engaged in their private devotions. Today many people experience time in church as primarily quiet time 'for me'.

Eucharist is only truly happening when it is something that we do together. If we all have multiple separate individual Eucharistic experiences, it is much the same as when multiple priests said multiple private Masses at multiple side altars. Connecting has to be horizontal as well as vertical, with my companions (literally) as well as with my God. We go to Mass to be together and to feel together – to connect with one another.

Koinonia

St Paul said, 'the bread that we break, is it not a sharing in the body of Christ?' (1 Corinthians 10:16). His word for sharing, *koinonia,* is often translated rather weakly as 'community'. 'Participation' might better render his sense. When we break bread, we are participating in the body of Christ.

This participating has the two meanings we have just outlined. It has the vertical meaning of my personal communion with Christ, my being in Christ and Christ being in me. And it has the horizontal meaning of our communion with one another as fellow members of the body of Christ. It does not make sense to experience one without the other or to think of one and not the other.

Mission

Besides celebrating and besides connecting, Eucharist is about mission. It is as if the Eucharist exerts a centrifugal as well as a centripetal force. It draws us in, to connect with the Lord. And then it pushes us away, it sends us, it 'missions' us.

But look how this too was lost in what we were previously habituated to. The old Latin Mass ended with the priest saying, *Ita missa est* – the same word as 'mission'. But we were used to thinking of it more as an ending than a sending. Today we hear the words, 'Go in peace to love and serve the Lord.' But in large part we continue to experience the final words as a conclusion, a wrapping up, not as a beginning and a commission.

Again, think of our traditions of fasting before Mass, how we fasted for one hour, three hours, since midnight even. And compare the words of Isaiah. The kind of fasting that God wants is fasting from injustice and participating in God's solidarity with the weak and oppressed (Isaiah 58). Somehow we reduced the practice of God's justice to a private, ritualistic observance, of little or no consequence to anybody else.

Bringing about God's justice, as I described it in a previous chapter, is the realisation of Eucharist. Without it, Eucharist remains not-yet-celebrated. If Eucharist exerts only a centripetal pull on me, I am only in receiving mode. If it exerts a centrifugal push, it sends me away. It turns the attention from my hunger to the hunger of the world, from fasting from food to fasting from injustice.

Variety

These perspectives – the themes of celebration and active involvement, of connecting and of mission, of the vertical and the horizontal – give a backdrop for exploring how to make the experience of Mass a strategic focus within pastoral planning. The focus is: How can our Eucharist truly be a connecting with God, a celebrating together, an impulse to mission?

For a start, I would point to the value of variety. This means, first of all, a variety of ministry – musicians, ministers of the

Word and Eucharist, greeters, servers, organisers, sacristy staff, cleaning and decorating teams, collectors and counters. Masses with a scarcity of such ministries are making a powerful negative statement.

Not alone should there be variety but it should be reinforced for people again and again. The variety of ministry is a statement that we are a ministering community, all called to active participation in the Eucharist and beyond. It is saying that we all here are doing this together.

Variety also means a variety of Masses in an area, or even in an individual parish if there are still a lot of Masses. Different people are drawn to different kinds of liturgy – traditional choir, younger people's music, quiet style of Mass, family Mass, *Aifreann Gaeilge*. Variety is attractive. It maximises the possibility of connecting with different people and different styles of spirituality.

A team

Some of the most life-giving Masses have a team who plan and co-ordinate the whole experience, with attention to detail and to quality. Many family Masses fall into this category. This provides a model in the effort to enhance the quality of all the weekend Masses. It strongly suggests that we can have the kind of Masses we need to have if we identify people who have the energy to drive the process.

A 'team' can be quite small, maybe no more than two or three people. But it is essential that the priest is actively engaged. The function, however, is not to 'provide for' people in a way that perpetuates passive participation. The ultimate role of a team is to generate a sense of ownership, where the whole community that comes for that Mass feels responsible for the quality of its celebration.

The same thinking applies outside Sunday. It applies to funeral Masses in a special way. It applies to Christmas. The huge scope for outreach seems to me to depend to a great extent on having a team of people who can creatively deliver on the potential.

Welcome

Welcome is as the heart of this approach. The team could well see their goal as one of bringing the celebration to a stage where a sense of welcome pervades the whole Mass. If there is a feeling of welcome people are already connecting with one another as the body of Christ. If there is a feeling of welcome, God's own welcome is already tangible.

Welcome is there from the start. There might be a welcoming face when people arrive at church. A procession should be the norm, to invite and draw all present into the celebration. If somebody other than the priest introduces the Mass, this will increase the sense that it is our Mass.

Welcome means a special effort to make the Word of God as accessible as possible. It sounds so obvious, but if the proclaiming is slow and clear people will feel at home. If it is not clear, people are being alienated from their own celebration.

Welcome also comes across in the prayers of the faithful. If they feel real and have a local relevance, people will feel at home. So often they are trite, hackneyed, clichéd, formal, reflecting nothing of the power of prayer.

Music especially has a power for welcome. It can bond people in the same Spirit, it can channel feeling. At the same time there is a big challenge to musicians to focus their gifts on participation mainly rather than performance solely. It is lovely to listen but we are most together when we are all singing.

The homily

The homily is a key focus of attention, given its potential for impacting on people. It is a considerable burden for one person to bear. It becomes near to unbearable if that person does not enjoy public speaking or if he is the only priest in the parish and therefore the only voice ever heard at homily time.

There are possibilities that can be explored. One is to involve lay people alongside the priest, so that people hear their own experience articulated by one like them. Occasional dialogue homilies could be part of this also. Another possibility is to have a weekly session of prayer and sharing around the following Sunday's gospel. This would allow the homily to be informed by people's reflections. There is also the possibility of priests from neighbouring parishes swapping places occasionally.

It may be unrealistic to imagine that every Eucharist, week in week out, would be a special experience. Is it? Maybe not. Much of the time we are at the other end of the scale where so many are felt to be routine and dull. Again it is our conditioning, going back generations. Mass is something we 'get'; everybody goes through their motions. But there are real possibilities for trans-formation.

Not just possibilities, but imperatives. It is not that every-thing depends on the Mass. A lot of it is about the quality of faith community that is generated beforehand. But so much hangs on this one event in the week. As I said at the start, it is not about transforming the Mass. It is about transforming ourselves, our familiarity, our complacency. It is about a new vitality in our wanting this precious time together.

CHAPTER 24

Care

Faith is in your head, it is in your heart, it is in your hands. In your head, it is your understanding of existence, centred on Christ's death and resurrection. In your heart it is your relationship to Jesus, how you trust in him and are captivated by him. In your hands it is what you do, helping to bring about God's kingdom.

There is nothing new about any of this, but there is a new appreciation today of the 'hands' aspect. Traditionally Catholic theology spoke about faith in 'head' language a lot of the time. It was even defined in terms of 'one's assent to revealed truths'. Part of Luther's Reformation was to re-emphasise the 'heart' aspect, where faith means entrusting all of ourselves to the Lord.

The contemporary sense of faith is that it manifests itself primarily in action. It is not enough to know what you believe. It is not enough to feel it in your heart. It must be lived. Apart from anything else, this is how the world will come to believe. As Paul VI put it: 'Modern people listen more willingly to witnesses than to teachers, and if they do listen to teachers, it is because they are witnesses.'

This means that faith community is, at its heart, about *doing*. It is a place where the vision is lived and it is lived principally through the practice of care. Caring is practical. It is practicable. It is possible for each person. It is instantly relevant and instantly recognisable. It is down to earth, yet it has extraordinary depth. In attending to the ministry of caring, the parish is in touch with its own profound identity.

Suffering

I recall one priest observing that suffering is the biggest question in life. His own experience of ministry had brought him into contact with all kinds of suffering – for instance, people who had been sick or housebound for years; tragic death, including that of a child or a young parent; families destroyed by violence or substance abuse; intense loneliness. Every example we would add to the list confirms his observation.

But it is even broader than that. I think that all of us suffer. It may be in ways that are less extreme but it is no less real. It may be that you cannot understand your children – or your parents. Or that you cannot find peace. Or that you feel you have wasted years. Or that you are carrying a burden. Or that you are looking for love. Or that you are trying too hard.

To call it 'suffering' might feel too indulgent, but that is what it is. We would imagine ourselves differently but to suffer and to be human are inseparable. The flipside of this, however, is that to care is quintessentially human. Care is the fundamental response to the human situation. In caring it is as if we declare our transcendence. The gospel would say that in caring we discover our divinity.

Welcome

In this light we can say that caring is the great ministry in the welcoming parish. It is the core practice of the ministering community. A welcoming parish expresses itself in many ways, as we have been seeing, but primarily through the exercise of care. What could be more welcoming than the sense that the faith community says to me, to me individually: 'We care that you exist'?

To be cared for is, first of all, to be noticed. When I am noticed I, who may have been just anybody at all as far as the faith community was concerned, become somebody. All the more so when I am noticed in my suffering. It is as if there are others who know my pain. It is a feeling of being brought in from the cold. It is a feeling of healing, which is also a feeling of being saved – a link that the Irish *slánaigh/slánú* suggestively makes for us.

Here it might be worth recalling that the first message of the gospel is not 'love one another'. The first message is that we are loved. And the first command of the gospel is: 'Allow yourself to be loved.' The parish is meant to be a place where everybody has this experience. People's first experience of parish should not be the commandment to love. It should be the experience of being cared for. That is the first thing God wishes to say to any of us.

A universal ministry

In the past, if we had thought about the ministry of caring in the parish we might have thought of the priest. His ministry was modelled on that of the good shepherd. He was there at the time of death and dying. He prayed with the sick. He comforted the troubled. He visited the prisoner.

The priest's presence in all this is as precious as ever. But today our understanding of this ministry has been expanded and enriched. We now see that it involves lay people as much as priests. Of course people always cared, but now parishioners are becoming more and more involved in a public ministry of caring in the name of the parish. Some of the innovations are acknowledged below.

But it is broader still. All public ministries, as I proposed earlier, are directed towards affirming and enabling the ministry of all, as part of the overall movement from a 'provided-for' church to a self-ministering church. The answer to, 'who does the caring ministry?' is not a special team but you and I, all of us. It is our human and Christian calling. The ministry arises out of our humanity and out of our faith.

This needs to be affirmed. Though there can never be enough caring, it is amazing how much caring goes on. It manifests itself at times of special need, such as tragedy or death. But – a constant refrain in these chapters – people often see no link between this deep human instinct and being a Christian.

When the parish affirms the caring that is going on, it helps people make the link. And when the link is made, parish itself has been changed. There is a growing awareness that the caring which most deeply engages us in our personal lives is also at the heart of what a parish is. When we see the link we have a feeling that we are parish.

Sacrament

The ministry of caring is a ministry that has a sacrament 'attached' to it, the sacrament of anointing. But the link between the sacrament and ordinary living is quite weak. What goes on in the sacrament goes on apart from what is going on in the daily life of the faith community.

Here I am thinking of a 'sacrament' as a kind of peak expression of something that is going on all the time in the faith community. The sacrament of reconciliation is meant to be a celebration of all the struggles in our daily life to practise the ministry of reconciliation, to confess and to forgive and to make good. Likewise the sacrament of anointing is meant to be a celebration of our ordinary experience of caring and healing in response to need and suffering.

We could actually feel this if the sacrament were celebrated reasonably often in a public way in the parish. To some extent this happens, on occasions such as a parish mission or novena or for world day of the sick. But it is not a lot. The sacrament can become a bigger part of the ongoing effort to communicate to all that caring is the ministry of all. The sacrament can become a celebration of the community, just as baptism is meant to become. It can then become a proclamation that the caring we exercise is the Word become flesh amongst us.

Illustrations

I imagine that in an ideal parish the public ministry of caring would be a tapestry of all kinds of initiatives in response to all kinds of needs. New needs keep emerging and unvoiced needs come to be noticed, so there would be an ever-changing pattern and an ever-sharpening sensitivity. The following initiatives are indicative of what is possible.

Ministers of the Eucharist may bring communion to people who are housebound or in nursing homes. When the ministers are sent from the Sunday Eucharist, it can raise the assembly's consciousness of its own calling to care. Again, when the Sunday Eucharist is made available by radio link, many who are housebound or sick feel greatly cared for and noticed.

Again, ministries around bereavement are a powerful expression of care. There may be a team whose members accompany those who are suffering bereavement. There may be a group that offers people – not just adults, but children also – a welcoming context in which to process their grief. These are among the most inspiring examples of what the ministry of caring can do.

A group might take it upon themselves to visit fellow parishioners who are sick or hospitalised, housebound or lonely. In some parishes there is a group to 'care for the carers'. They give a break to those whose day is absorbed in caring for a family member. In the process they show that they notice the pain of the carer and not only that of the invalid.

Caring is two-way

The parish can take it from there by asking itself questions such as: Who is suffering amongst us? Who is needing to be noticed? Who is calling forth our care? There is just one further point I would add and it concerns the vocation to care of the person who is being or has been cared for.

We speak today of the 'wounded healer'. It is a recognition that the person suffering is not just passive, not just to be ministered to. That person is still a gift for others. The ministry of care is not dependent on being healthy. Even in their indigence people minister, not just by their prayers, but by their presence, their courage, their suffering.

John Paul II suggests that we think of the suffering individual 'not simply as an object of the church's love and service, but as an active and responsible participant in the work of evangelisation and salvation'. The faith community needs to open itself to be evangelised by the suffering in its own body. It needs to explicitly welcome and celebrate this ministry in its own midst.

Sometimes the ministry of care is shared between people who have the same experience in common. It has been called 'like-to-like' ministry. Those who have suffered loss are ministered to by people who themselves have been bereaved. Somebody who is sick is shown care by another who has had the same affliction. And so on. Often a person feels best understood by somebody who has 'been there' themselves. Often people are drawn to a ministry of care out of their own experience of suffering.

Identity

Caring is bigger than the church. This becomes evident when you try to list all the caring initiatives that go on in the parish. Some of them are coming from a church source and some of them are community based. Cancer support, AA, meals on wheels sit alongside the parish bereavement team and the Vincent de Paul.

All of them are equally valuable. Care is care whether the motivation is deeply human or deeply Christian. It is similar work. It is a similar passion. This suggests that the ministry of care in the parish has a further dimension. Beyond the actual care itself, there is the potential for building bridges, for reaching out, for linking with others in a common cause.

Not so long ago this could not have been conceived of. 'Parish' and 'community' were the same thing. They ran into one another. Nowadays this is less and less the case. More and more, 'parish' is an element within a larger community that includes lots of people who do not profess the Christian religion and lots of services that do not have a Christian inspiration.

This raises questions of identity for the parish. How is it to define itself in this new context? What is its particular niche? What is distinctive about the care it practises? The question is not meant in the sense of 'we're different'. It is meant in the sense of getting in touch with our own deep and distinguishing motivation. Then we can hope to care more explicitly and more deliberately out of what we are.

Kingdom

God's Spirit is bigger than the church. As St John says, 'the wind blows where it chooses' (John 3:8). God's Spirit is moving in all kinds of ways. It cannot be corralled in by the church, so as to control its movement. The church is forever challenged to advert to the new and surprising ways in which the Spirit works in the world.

Another word for this is kingdom. 'Kingdom' is Jesus' word for God's passion, for what God wants for God's people, the reign of God's loving-kindness and peace and rightness. Kingdom is not far off. It is already happening whenever God's dream is taking shape – whenever care is practised. And that is much bigger than church.

The faith community could choose to become a kind of spiritual oasis. It could choose to see the 'outside' world as hostile. It choose to regard itself as the possessor of the truth and in no need of listening. But that would be to lose rather than monopolise God's Spirit, who is alive in all human caring.

Hopefully it would choose instead to recognise the potential for partnership. It would see, first of all, the common ground. Christians share with many others a commitment to the human cause. They can find common ground with others in the community in the aspiration to a fuller humanity and a more human togetherness in the world.

It can do this if it thinks 'Spirit' and 'kingdom' and not just 'church'. The world is the scene of God's saving activity, God's kingdom-shaping, God's Spirit acting. The faith community can rejoice that all kinds of people are partners in God's work in all kinds of ways, however they themselves might describe it. More than rejoice, it can open itself to be evangelised by this unexpected witness.

While stepping forward to stand on this common ground of care, the faith community is also growing in awareness of where it itself is coming from. It has a language and a ritual coming out of the gospels, whereby it can see how the Spirit stirs up desire for kingdom in the very desire for fuller humanity. It can appreciate that whenever people care they are not just realising their humanity. They are entering into their divinity.

References

CHAPTER 1: WHY PARISH?

Page 9   'I believe that this old and respected structure' (Pope Paul VI); quoted in John Paul II, *The Vocation and Mission of the Lay Faithful* (1988), 26.

Page 11   'Not principally a structure'; John Paul II, *The Vocation and Mission of the Lay Faithful*, 26.

Page 14   'One of the few open communities'; Allan White, 'Seeking a Theology of the Parish,' *Priests and People*, April 1991, 133.

CHAPTER 2: THE LAST SUPPER

Page 20   'This is the story'; I am indebted to Jan Coll for this story.

CHAPTER 3: A MINISTERING COMMUNITY

Page 25   'Solidarity is about the duty of all'; John Paul II, *The Church's Social Concern* (1987), 38.

Page 27   'The members of the Body of Christ should recognise themselves'; Cardinal Mahony, *As I Have Done for You: A Pastoral Letter on Ministry* (Los Angeles Diocese, 2000), part three.

Page 28   'If you wish to understand'; Augustine, Sermon 272.

CHAPTER 4: WELCOME

Page 34   'What he calls the new evangelisation'; John Paul II, *The Church's Missionary Mandate* (1990), 33.

Page 34   'We need a mission-centred church'; David Bosch, *Transforming Mission: Paradigm Shifts in the Theology of Mission* (Maryknoll: Orbis, 1991), 370.

Page 35   'In our day, what has happened'; Paul VI, *Evangelisation in the Modern World* (1975), 4.

CHAPTER 5: A FEELING OF HOME

Page 37   This is a revised version of a chapter that appeared in a previous book of mine, *What is Morality?* (Columba, 1996).

Page 39   'A house of welcome for all'; John Paul II, *The Vocation and Mission of the Lay Faithful*, 27.

Page 132 'This is the idea in the RCIA; *Rite of Christian Initiation of Adults,* 138.

Page 135 'The words of Paul VI'; *Evangelisation in the Modern World,* 71.

CHAPTER 17: ADULT FAITH

Page 137 'The split between the gospel and culture'; Paul VI, *Evangelisation in the Modern World,* 20.

Page 141 'Church documents today are re-affirming the priority'; John Paul II, *Catechesis in Our Time* (1979), 43.

CHAPTER 18: THE MINISTRY OF THE WORD

Page 146 'The Church has always venerated'; Vatican II, *Constitution on Revelation,* 21.

Page 147 'The first task of priests'; Vatican II, *Decree on the Ministry and Life of Priests,* 4.

Page 147 'The people of God is formed into one'; Vatican II, *Decree on the Ministry and Life of Priests,* 4.

Page 148 'The one who has learned to live a new life'; Augustine, Sermon 34.

Page 150 'Access to Scripture'; Vatican II, *Constitution on Divine Revelation,* 22.

Page 150 'Ignorance of the Scriptures'; St Jerome, Prologue to the Commentary on Isaiah.

Page 155 'Beannú Ministéirí'; I am indebted to Caitlín Ní Chatháin for this translation.

CHAPTER 19: JUSTICE MINISTRY IN THE PARISH

Page 160 'The ache of God'; Walter Brueggemann, *The Prophetic Imagination* (Philadelphia: Fortress Press, 1978), 59. I am indebted to this book for its reflections on the themes of numbness and compassion.

Page 163 'Solidarity is not a feeling of vague compassion'; John Paul II, *The Church's Social Concern,* 38.

CHAPTER 23: MASS MINISTRY

Page 193 'It is your own mystery'; Augustine, Sermon 272.

CHAPTER 24: CARE

Page 199   'Modern people listen more willingly'; Paul VI, *Evangelisation in the Modern World*, 41.

Page 203   'Not simply as an object'; John Paul II, *The Vocation and Mission of the Lay Faithful*, 54.